THE TRUTH OF HAPPINESS

COURSE

JOHN HASPEL

THE TRUTH OF HAPPINESS *COURSE*

A ten-week study of meditation and mindfulness from the Buddha's direct teachings for developing a life of lasting peace and happiness

John Haspel

Simple Enlightenment Press

Questions, Comments or Newsletter Subscriptions please use the contact form at CrossRiverMeditation.com

Dedication

This book is dedicated to my Sangha at the Cross River Meditation Center in Frenchtown New Jersey. Thank you all for your mindful presence, enlightening discussions, and for the precious honor of being your teacher.

To the true Refuge of The Three Jewels:
The Buddha, The Dhamma and The Sangha.

Acknowledgements

To Moira Kowalczyk for your inspiration and the many enlightening discussions that brought clarity. Thank You.

To Deb Kolar for her invaluable assistance with proofing and with contextual clarity. Thank You.

To Lorna Mcginlay for her assistance with the Glossary. Thank You.

This book was developed with Scrivener, finished with Pages, and formatted for digital publication with Jutoh

About revisions to this book:

This book was first published for distribution in September of 2014. This first revision was published in September of 2015 that includes correction of grammatical and punctuation errors, a reorganization of certain content, and additional content on impermanence and the ego-self.

There is also an extensive re-write for the chapters on Dependent Origination and The Five Clinging-Aggregates, and the following chapter on Kamma and Rebirth.

One of the most humbling and rewarding aspects of teaching the Buddha's Dhamma are the questions and feedback from the students in my classes and from many of those who have taken this course online. All have been instrumental in the revisions presented here. Please continue with your questions and comments.

Being mindful of the uncertainties of anicca, I will likely continue with future revisions. Peace.

John Haspel, September 2015

Contents

Introduction

This book is written as an individual Dhamma study and as a ten-week online correspondence course. As an individual Dhamma study it is a comprehensive introduction to the Buddha's path of developing lasting peace and happiness.

If you have not subscribed to the course and you would like to take this course with my insight and guidance, please go to: http://crossrivermeditation.com.

The teachings of the Buddha have profoundly changed my life. It has been over 2,500 years since the Buddha first presented the Dhamma yet these teachings continue to be available and accessible in their original form. That the original and authentic teachings are still available today shows the power of the Buddha's direct teachings to maintain purity and relevancy even with continual adaptations and accommodations.

Modern Buddhism has taken on many different forms from the original teachings. As the teachings of the Buddha spread from a small corner of Northern India, the teachings were influenced by many individuals and the cultures, beliefs and social climate that they developed in. Modern Buddhism is as diverse as the individual interpretations and the cultures these teachings passed through.

I studied in many of the later developed traditions most often referred to as the Mahayana schools of Buddhism. I have found the individual and cultural influences that have impacted these schools to be confusing and at times misleading.

The more esoteric, mystical, and magical the teachings of the Buddha became, the more difficult it became to integrate these teachings. Even the idea that these teachings are difficult to understand develop seemed contrary to what the Buddha intended.

The Dhamma is often presented today as an impossible goal that will take "limitless eons" to achieve. This notion simply creates more confusion and develops a state of mind that is constantly grasping.

If the Buddha's sole purpose was to bring an end to stress, unhappiness and confusion, why would his path be nearly impossible to understand, and often create additional confusion?

I came to see that much of my confusion was arising from the individual and culturally-influenced adaptations and accommodations to the Buddha's original teachings. When I put aside the more esoteric, magical, and mystical teachings that developed after the Buddha's death, and began to study the Buddha's direct teachings, these simple and profound teachings became understandable, useful, and effective.

Buddhism adapted to various cultures within a framework of each culture's beliefs and held views. I believe the difficulty that many Westerners have had in integrating the Dhamma is in attempting to develop an understanding of the Dhamma from the perspective of an unfamiliar culture.

As Buddhism moved to the West, with a much more pragmatic view of the world, many Westerners attempted to integrate the teachings AND the cultural influences already present. With no perspective in which to understand the cultural influences, great confusion has arisen. This has led to the original teachings to be shrouded in mystery, hidden behind dogma and ritual, and lacking the context in which the original teachings were presented.

The Buddha did not intend his teachings to be useful only for those with the right lineage, the right kamma, the right teacher, the right empowerment, the right social position, or the right culture.

The Buddha taught a simple and direct path of developing lasting peace and happiness. This teaching is accessible and understandable to anyone who takes to the Dhamma whole-heartedly. In this study there will be no analysis of concepts nor an attempt to prove the validity of the Buddha's teachings within any tradition that developed after the Buddha's death. I will explain terms as I understand them and as supported in the Pali Canon.

I will, by necessity, and intending Right Speech, show where adaptations and accommodations to the Buddha's original teachings have occurred and become generally accepted as "Buddhist" teachings. I intend no disrespect to any tradition, school or Buddhist religion. I intend only clarity and a useful Dhamma.

The Buddha taught freedom from the delusion of stress and the underlying unsatisfactoriness of life common to all. He taught that freedom, or awakening, can be achieved in this present lifetime.

I hold great reverence for all of the various Buddhist religions and schools that have developed since the passing of the Buddha. Many people have found meaning and purpose through these individually and culturally influenced adaptations.

I have found through my own direct inquiry that the teachings of the Buddha as preserved in the Pali Canon are most effective in developing the Buddha's stated purpose.

In the Simsapa Sutta the Buddha describes the purpose of his teachings:

"And what have I taught? 'I teach the nature of dukkha (stress). I teach the origination of dukkha (craving and clinging originate dukkha). I teach that cessation of dukkha is possible. I teach that The Eightfold Path is the path leading to the cessation of dukkha: This is what I have taught.

"And why have I taught these things? Because they are connected with the goal. They relate to the rudiments of the mindful life. These teachings develop disenchantment and dispassion. These

17

teachings develop cessation of stress and unhappiness. They bring calm, and direct knowledge. These teachings develop self-awakening and unbinding. This is why I have taught them.

"Therefore your practice is contemplating and understanding: 'This is stress... This is the origination of stress... This is the cessation of stress.' Your practice is contemplating and understanding: 'This is the path of practice leading to the cessation of stress." [1]

All Sutta citations are from the Pali Canon and are listed in Endnotes at the end of this book.

The original teachings of the Buddha are the most practical teachings for developing lasting peace and happiness still present in the world today. These teachings are presented to end all suffering in this lifetime. The purpose of this book and this course is to present the original teachings of the Buddha in a direct and useful manner.

This ten-week course will present Shamatha-Vipassana meditation within the context of an ancient and profound teaching known as The Four Noble Truths. The Four Noble Truths are the Buddha's teachings on the underlying unsatisfactory nature of human life and the cause of unsatisfactory experiences. By developing understanding of the unsatisfactory nature of life and the cause of all stress and unhappiness, a life of lasting peace and happiness can be developed.

The Buddha's teachings on The Four Noble Truths and the supporting teachings are known as the "Dhamma."

Dhamma is a Pali word that means truth or truthful teachings of the Buddha and is based entirely on the Pali Canon. The more common word dharma refers to teachings in the Mahayana schools of Buddhism and is based in part on additional texts that developed after the life of the Buddha.

The Buddha often stated: "Both formerly & now, for all time, it is only stress (Dukkha) that I describe, and the cessation of stress." [2]

The Buddha taught only one subject: The origination of stress and the cessation of stress. He taught this one subject for the most compassionate of reasons. He wanted human beings to find real and lasting happiness in this present human life and in this present environment. The teachings of the Buddha are often misunderstood as pessimistic. The First Noble Truth is a realistic understanding of the nature of a human being's life experience. The result of realistically facing the problem of delusion and unhappiness is the ability to develop wisdom and lasting peace and happiness.

The Buddha's awakening brought understanding of the cause of unsatisfactoriness and a path leading to lasting happiness. The Buddha taught that the cause of the underlying unsatisfactory nature of life is ignorance, or a lack of understanding. This is a very specific ignorance, ignorance of The Four Noble Truths, that leads to the unsatisfying experience of life.

Due to a lack of understanding an ego-self that is prone to clinging is formed. This ego-self is referred to as non-self or not-self throughout the Buddhist literature. I will explain not-self in detail in weeks seven and eight.

To end the suffering of not-self the Buddha taught Four Noble Truths:

1. The Truth of Dukkha (unsatisfactoriness, disappointment, suffering, stress)

2. The Truth of the Origination of Suffering

   (clinging, craving)

3. The Truth of the Cessation of Suffering

4. The Truth of the Path Leading to the Cessation of Suffering

To reiterate, the Buddha's sole purpose for teaching was to bring lasting peace and happiness to all who would whole-heartedly engage his Dhamma. The Buddha's Dhamma does not include anything that does not directly develop his stated purpose, or would likely lead to further confusion.

He did not teach anything that further distracted an already confused mind. The Buddha understood that teaching any subject that created further confusion would have been cruel. History has shown the Buddha to be the world's most refined and insightful thinker and the essence of compassion informed by true wisdom.

He consistently refused to answer questions on subjects such as eternalism, infinite versus finite existence, transmigration of a "soul," what the "self" might be, and many more questions that would only cause additional confusion and distract from liberation.

21

Shamatha-Vipassana meditation is the method of meditation that the Buddha taught for the forty-five years of his teaching the Dhamma.

Shamatha is a Pali word meaning tranquility or calm and Vipassana is a Pali word meaning insight or to gain insight to. Shamatha-Vipassana meditation is a meditation method of gently developing a mind-state of tranquility and calm so that you are no longer distracted by your own thoughts. Once your mind achieves a measure of tranquility, you are able to gain insight into your mind and insight into your thoughts, words and deeds that contribute to stress, confusion and unhappiness.

It should be noted here that the Buddha did not intend to develop a religion or worship. He did not create a doctrine to be followed blindly. Put aside any ideas you may have of the Buddha as a religious, supernatural, or mystical being. The Buddha was simply a human being who, through his own effort and investigation, "awakened" to these truths. (Buddha means awakened)

The Buddha taught a simple and straightforward method of understanding the truth of lasting peace and happiness. The path leading to lasting peace and happiness is The Eightfold Path.

Shamatha-Vipassana meditation is one factor of The Eightfold Path.

The Eightfold Path can be developed by anyone regardless of current religious practice. Some established religions have much fear arising from misunderstanding meditation and the investigation of the nature of stress and unhappiness. The Eightfold Path can be developed by anyone seeking a more meaningful life, or simply a practical way of understanding themselves on a deep and profound level.

As a practice, what is learned in this course is to be practiced. There is nothing in The Four Noble Truths or The Eightfold Path that has any magical qualities of bringing instant understanding. The meditation method used in this course is most effective when developed within the framework of The Eightfold Path. The Eightfold Path provides the perspective, structure and direction necessary for lasting peace and happiness to be experienced.

A basic concept of this course and Shamatha-Vipassana meditation is mindfulness. Mindfulness means to recollect and to hold in mind. By developing an understanding of the causes of stress and unhappiness we can then be mindful, or to recollect and hold in mind, the practice leading to lasting happiness. The Four Foundations of Mindfulness are presented in the second week of this course to develop mindfulness within your meditation practice.

Despite modern references to "mindfulness meditation," shamatha-vipassana meditation is practiced primarily to develop concentration. Mindfulness then is a refined quality of mind that is developed from concentration and direct application of these teachings.

The problem of stress and unhappiness is that stress creates a constant distraction in our minds. Distraction is a lack of concentration and mindfulness. As human beings we become preoccupied with grasping after that which brings pleasure and we become preoccupied with avoiding that which is unpleasant or disappointing. With some, preoccupation rises to the level of psychosis and compulsion or addiction.

By developing a tranquil mind allowing for insight to arise, our minds become more focused and less distracted. A deep and abiding mindfulness of life as life occurs is developed. We are no longer distracted by grasping and avoidance. With Dhamma practice, lasting peace and happiness is realized.

We will begin in week one with learning the basic practice of Shamatha-Vipassana meditation. The following weeks will develop an understanding of meditation within the context and supportive framework of The Four Noble Truths and The Eightfold Path.

This ten-week course will develop an understanding of the impermanent and uncertain environment that contributes to stress and unhappiness and use this understanding to deepen mindfulness and develop abiding peace and happiness. The direct teachings of the Buddha will be developed and integrated through study and the practical application of concentration and refined mindfulness.

Week ten will be focused on recognizing common hindrances to establishing and maintaining a Dhamma practice within the framework of The Eightfold Path and establishing a life-long practice of mindfulness of the Buddha's Dhamma.

These lessons are simple and straightforward. The understanding developed is up to you to integrate into your life. A certain amount of time is necessary each day to establish a meditation and mindfulness practice, though not an impossible amount. You may even find that once your mind begins to quiet and you make choices that are more mindful, you have more time for what is most important to you.

The distraction of stress and unhappiness will be left behind and a deep and abiding mindfulness of peace and happiness will prevail.

At the end of each chapter is a guideline for your Dhamma practice each week and integrating these teachings. I recommend that you take this course as intended, one lesson a week, or longer. Take your time.

If you feel you need to review a week or spend more then one week on each chapter lesson, please do so. Do not expect too much of yourself from the start. Be gentle with yourself. Don't judge yourself, your practice, or the Dhamma harshly.

If taking the correspondence course there is a brief writing assignment at the end of each week. The purpose of the assignment is to review your developing understanding and to ask any questions related to this Dhamma course. After week five and week ten you will have the opportunity for a phone conversation with me. The email address that you used when you signed up for this course will be your initial point of contact.

Whether you are subscribed to the correspondence course, or not, as a student of this course please feel free to email me with any questions or comments at john@crossrivermeditation.com.

I have found the most useful and effective Buddhist teachings to be those that are direct teachings of the Buddha. This book is based entirely on theses direct teachings.

A Sutta is a direct teaching of the Buddha as preserved in the Pali Canon. I will occasionally include a relevant Sutta for context. The Sutta's cited are listed in the Endnotes section at the back of this book. The direct teachings from the Pali Canon are in quotes. All online links (Electronic Editions) to the suttas are from the website http://www.accesstoinsight.org and are included here according to their posted copyright and Creative Commons License.

All translations of the Pali Canon are at least partially interpretive based on the translator's understanding of the intent and context of the subject matter. I have also made slight changes in the direct translations for clarity in the context presented.

What is of primary importance for any translation of the Pali Canon is to maintain authenticity with the consistent teachings presented in the canon. The translations of Thanissaro Bikkhu reflect his profound understanding of these texts and have been most useful to me.

A note about terminology: The word that the Buddha used to describe stress is Dukkha. Dukkha also can be translated to mean unsatisfactoriness, disappointment, disillusionment, disenchantment, suffering and confusion. I will use the words unsatisfactory, disappointment, disenchantment, unhappiness, and stress interchangeably to signify all manifestations of Dukkha.

I will repeat certain concepts within different contexts. This is done for both clarity and emphasis as the entire Dhamma relates to the cessation of stress and unhappiness within the context of The Four Noble Truths. This is similar to how the Buddha presented his teachings.

For forty-five years the Buddha taught only the truth of Dukkha and the truth of the cessation of Dukkha. His teachings are preserved in the second book of the Pali Canon known as the Sutta Pitaka or the collection of the Buddha's teachings. His first Sutta, The Dhammacakkappavattana Sutta taught The Four Noble Truths and set the wheel of truth in motion. The remainder of his teachings support and explain this first teaching.

I will refer to the Buddha and his teachings throughout this book. This is not to set him apart or to elevate him to unrealistic stature as a savior or supreme being, something he refused to do as well. The references to the Buddha and the examples of his life should be taken in the context of him being a human being. He awakened as a human being and taught a way for all human beings to awaken.

Ehipassiko is a word often used by the Buddha. It means "come and see for yourself." Please, come and see for yourself.

Always be gentle with yourself.

John Haspel, September, 2014, September 2015

How To Use
This Dhamma Study

- Read the entire week's chapter
- Listen to the recording for each week's study (listed at the end of each chapter)
- Begin to integrate the week's teaching
- If taking the correspondence course: At the end of your week's practice submit your weekly course writing. Instructions are at the end of each chapter.

Take longer than a week for any chapter, or to review a chapter, if you feel this will be helpful in developing your understanding.

Week One
Shamatha-Vipassana
Meditation

If you have not read the course introduction, please do so now.

"Whatever is to be done by a teacher with compassion for the welfare of students, that has been done by me out of compassion for you. Here are the roots of trees. Here are empty places. Go and meditate. Don't be lazy. Don't become one who is later remorseful. This is my instruction to you." [3]

The purpose of this course is to understand stress and disappointment and their cause. Once the cause of unhappiness is understood it can be mindfully abandoned. Shamatha-Vipassana meditation is the technique that you will use to develop concentration and insight. Concentration and insight brings recognition of how you create stress and unhappiness. Finally, concentration develops the useful mindfulness to abandon all causes of stress and unhappiness.

The meditation technique that you will learn and practice in this course is the same meditation technique used by Siddartha Gautama, a human being, who would become the Buddha. Shamatha is a Pali word which means calm abiding, tranquility, serenity or quiet. Vipassana is a Pali word which means insight or to gain insight.

Once your mind is settled and tranquil, free of the distraction of its own compulsive thoughts, insight into unhappiness and stress, its cause and its cessation arises. Using this method of meditation along with the other seven factors of The Eightfold Path, Siddartha Gautama achieved the cessation of stress and "awakened" to a fully mindful state free of craving, clinging and continual self-identification.. He became the Buddha.

Pali is the language most closely associated with the Buddha's language and Pali is the language of the original texts recording the direct teachings of the Buddha. Dukkha is a Pali word that has a broad meaning including stress, unsatisfactory, disappointment, disillusionment, disenchantment, suffering and unhappiness. I will use the terms dukkha, stress and unhappiness interchangeably.

Sukkha is a Pali word whose meaning is lasting happiness and human flourishing. It is the intention of this course to show you how to develop lasting happiness and to flourish in your life.

The most debilitating effect of stress is the distraction that stress causes. A mind distracted will constantly seek stimulation, feeding its own distracted state. This constant need for stimulation manifests in many ways. You live in a world that provides unlimited opportunities for distraction and compulsive and addictive behavior. A well-concentrated mind will settle in mindfulness, free of the distraction of stress.

Meditation is typically listed as the eighth factor of The Eightfold Path. It is listed last to point out the importance that the other seven factors have in supporting a practice of meditation. Without the framework of The Eightfold Path, meditation is not likely to achieve the cessation of unhappiness and stress. Without developing mindfulness of all of your thoughts, words and deeds, your mind will remain too distracted for meditation to have any real and lasting effect.

You will learn the Shamatha-Vipassana meditation technique this week and use it to develop an understanding of the entire framework of The Eightfold Path.

The focus of this first lesson in meditation is to prepare the foundation for a lifetime of mindful practice within the mutually supportive framework of the Eightfold Path. Mindfulness is a subject you will spend two weeks on (week two and again in week six). For now it is enough to understand that the original teachings, and this course, are only concerned with mindfulness as mindfulness supports cessation of stress and the development of deep concentration.

Mindfulness means to "recollect" or to "hold in mind." This is a gentle holding in mind, though. Mindfulness is a quality of mind that develops gradually as distractions are lessened and concentration develops. Initially, you train your mind to put aside thoughts that distract. Concentration supports the useful mindfulness necessary in developing the Eightfold Path. Ultimately, mindfulness is the non-reactive quality of an awakened mind resting peacefully as life occurs.

As you progress, be mindful of recognizing thoughts and thought-constructs that create stress, unhappiness and confusion. Be mindful of thoughts or thought constructs that maintain or develop strong attachments to people, objects, events, or views. As you progress be mindful of thoughts or thought constructs that distract your mind to the past or to the future.

Remember, mindfulness is a gentle awareness of what your mind is presenting moment by moment. Let go of the need to analyze or evaluate thoughts or thought constructs including placing blame. This will only cause more distraction and add to stress. Mindfulness is a dispassionate observation of thoughts and events.

A point to be made here: Shamatha-Vipassana meditation is not for finding escape from your problems or generating magical or mystical experiences. The purpose of Shamatha-Vipassana meditation is to develop deep and abiding concentration and put aside all distractions caused by stress. Anything that would distract your mind will not support the practice of ending dukkha.

As you progress you will be able to verify the effectiveness of this practice yourself. This is a key point. There is nothing in the original teachings of the Buddha, or in this course, that implies anything magical or mystical will take place. It is through your direct efforts that change, profound change, will take place, if you apply yourself whole-heartedly.

You will develop an understanding that what is generated in your mind will profoundly and directly effect your life experience. This is why quieting your mind and gaining insight to your thoughts is so effective in changing your life experience and eliminating dukkha.

Meditation is practiced within the environment of impermanence. You will deepen your understanding of impermanence in a few weeks. (Week seven) For now, be mindful that the entirety of your life is taking place within an impermanent or ever-changing environment. Birth, aging and death are all experiences of impermanence. All of life's fleeting events along the way are also impermanent.

The distraction of stress occurs within this environment. Cessation of the distraction of stress occurs within this environment, too. This course and the meditation practice developed all occur within this environment. Impermanence, or more precisely, not recognizing impermanence or misunderstanding impermanence, allows for stress and unhappiness to develop and continue.

As you begin your meditation practice you will become mindful of thoughts and thought constructs attached to people, objects, events, views, and ideas that are distracting you. Notice that these thoughts are often focused on past or future events. Notice also that whatever is being held in mind at the moment is impermanent. Your thoughts are subject to the same impermanence as all other phenomenon.

It is important to note here the significant difference between a thought that directs to proper and appropriate thoughts and behavior and thought that develops additional stress and distraction. Understanding that it is time to get out of bed, make a phone call, take a pill, and all the other in-the-present-moment decisions you make are all entirely appropriate. Taking prudent action and thoughtful planning for the future is entirely appropriate. Reconsidering past events is entirely appropriate and can also develop insight.

Preoccupation with any thoughts or thought constructs creates additional stress and continues a distracted mind state. Expecting that which is inherently impermanent, including ourselves to somehow become permanent creates additional stress and continues a distracted mind state.

Thoughts which seek to establish and perpetuate an ego-self will continue to create unhappiness, disappointment, and stress.

The breath is used as a focus of concentration. Being mindful of the sensation of breathing while remaining non-distracted by your own thoughts is the essence of meditation. Initially in practice it is enough to put aside thoughts as they arise and return your awareness to your breath as soon as you realize you are attached to your thinking again. Very quickly using mindfulness of your breath, a quiet mind will develop. Without first quieting your mind you will have no useful mindfulness of thoughts necessary for insight.

The purpose of Shamatha-Vipassana meditation is to quiet your mind gaining concentration allowing for insight to arise. It is not the purpose of Shamatha-Vipassana meditation to create a forced mind state where no thoughts are discernible. With a forced mind state of nothingness what will be achieved is nothing, and not insight into stress and unhappiness.

You are a conscious being and thoughts should be flowing. The purpose of shamatha-vipassana is to not be distracted by your own thoughts.

If you are continuously following one thought with another thought, there is no spaciousness within your thoughts for developing insight. You are stuck in a compulsive mental state of immediately following one thought with the next.

Once you have the beginnings of a quiet mind, you can now gain insight into your thoughts. Now, with a quiet mind, you can stay with a thought or feeling for a moment or two, realizing the impermanence of all things and gaining further insight into the impermanence of all things including your own thoughts.

You can do this with any persistent thought or thought-construct or physical feeling. This is gaining true insight into conditioned thinking and diminishing the reaction caused by conditioned thinking.

Conditioned thoughts are thought constructs or thought patterns that have formed in your mind as reactions to events. The ego or ego-self is the result of conditioned thinking.

Shamatha-Vipassana meditation will return your mind to a permanent tranquil state not subject to reaction caused by wrong perception. Wrong perception, or wrong view, is caused by conditioned thinking.

Present conditioned thinking, or thought constructs, is formed from previously reactive thoughts. As will be seen, a reactive mind is a mind that is experiencing life from a perspective that arises from clinging, grasping and aversion.

Briefly, conditioned thinking causes ongoing wrong perception (wrong view) which causes an unskillful reaction which creates further conditioned thinking, and on and on. By using the tranquility and insight gained by Shamatha-Vipassana meditation you are letting go of reactive thoughts and interrupting the cycle of discursive conditioned thinking. This will be more clearly understood as your meditation practice develops.

No further analysis of your reactive thoughts or feelings is necessary, or even effective in breaking this pattern. Taking an overly analytical approach during meditation can often strengthen condition thinking due to the tranquil nature of your mind during meditation, leading to more conditioned thinking. At best, using meditation practice for deep analysis of conditioned thinking becomes simply another way of focusing on what caused conditioned thinking in the first place.

If you have the unskillful view that you are engaging in your meditation practice in order to "fix" yourself, or for grasping after pleasant mind states or mystical experiences, you will spend eternity in this pursuit, constantly creating the perception of change and never realizing the pure and unbound nature of your mind. The purpose of Shamatha-Vipassana meditation is to develop deep concentration and useful insight.

A mind easily distracted will be unable to recognize conditioned mind states. Conditioned mind arises and is reinforced by discriminating thoughts of wanting to hold onto what brings pleasure and wanting avoid what brings disappointment, pain and suffering. Conditioned mind is the vehicle used by your ego-personality to continue its hold over your life.

The concentration developed by Shamatha-Vipassana quickly develops the ability to recognize discursive and delusional thinking. Recognition of discursive and delusional thinking allows for the possibility of putting aside the cause of the stress and confusion that would otherwise continue to generate endless conditioned mind states.

The Buddha likened establishing a meditation practice to taming a wild elephant. In order for a young elephant to be useful, it must be able to focus and be aware of its true nature. To tame a young elephant, a strong rope would be tied around the elephant's neck and to a strong post or tree. The elephant would immediately begin thrashing around, flapping its ears, stomping the ground, and making loud grunts and bellows, very unhappy to not be able to wander around aimlessly engaging in any distraction that arose.

The more resistant the young elephant became, the stronger the rope held. Eventually the elephant would put aside its desire for continual distraction and sensual fulfillment and settle down.

In this metaphor, your mind is like the young elephant, the rope is mindfulness of your breath, and the strong post or tree is your breath. As you use mindfulness of your breath to disengage from your thoughts and settle your mindfulness on what is occurring, putting aside desire, you become liberated and free. By utilizing the simple method of Shamatha-Vipassana meditation you are able to tame your own wild mind.

As you begin to establish your meditation practice, your mind is often thrashing about, resistant to settling down. Thoughts insist on wandering aimlessly with strong desire to continue distraction by following one thought with another, continually describing their own self-created reality. As you continue and deepen your meditation practice, your thoughts settle down.

Returning to our metaphor, once the elephant has learned to remain mindful of the post, the rope is loosened and the elephant is finally free. Once you learn mindfulness of your breath and put aside the need to follow one thought with the next, you are finally free to begin the process of gaining insight into your mind.

As you let go of the need to describe reality based on desirous thoughts driven by attachment and aversion, you begin to develop true mindfulness. You put aside all that distracts you from lasting peace and happiness.

Acceptance and understanding of The Four Noble Truths, and practicing the first seven factors of The Eightfold Path begins to clear what are called "fetters" or "hindrances," agitated mind states which can make shamatha, quieting the mind, much more difficult, if not impossible.

The Four Noble Truths are explained in week three and The Eightfold Path is explained beginning in week four.

As you develop the complete framework of the Eightfold Path you are better able to benefit from Right Meditation. Remaining mindful of your moral and ethical behavior, and a practical application of your initial understanding of the Buddha's path, your meditation practice becomes more enjoyable and more effective. You are now more likely to continue a regular Dhamma practice.

The Buddha taught an Eightfold Path. Engaging in one aspect of the path, meditation, will not develop the skillful understanding necessary to awakening.

As you sit in meditation, focusing on the sensation of breathing, dispassionately putting aside thoughts as they arise, you naturally reach a state of tranquility. Conditioned thoughts and concepts will cease to cause a reaction in your thinking. You will gain true insight into conditioned mind and the impermanence of all thoughts.

True insight simply means recognizing impermanent thoughts and concepts as conditioned thinking. With dispassionate mindfulness you gently put thoughts aside, and gently return your mindfulness to your breath.

This simple but profound practice is now interrupting your clinging conditioned mind. Practicing shamatha-vipassana meditation within the framework of the Eightfold Path you are developing the ability to direct your thoughts rather than having your thinking direct your life.

direct?

Mindfulness is the ability to dispassionately hold in mind and remain distraction-free and aware of what is occurring.

Off your cushion your mindfulness becomes refined and you are less reactive to your conditioned thinking. You begin to integrate a deeper understanding of impermanence and your ego-self and you are more mindfully present in life as life occurs. Mindfulness can now support your meditation practice.

This simple and direct practice, free of the embellishments often placed on the Buddha's teaching, will gently lead to quieting your mind and developing a stress-free life of lasting peace and happiness. Shamatha-Vipassana is the foundation of a self-awareness practice that develops true liberation and freedom from dukkha.

Shamatha-Vipassana Meditation

Shamatha-Vipassana meditation is the method of meditation the Buddha used for his own awakening and the only meditation method that he taught throughout his 45 years of teaching the Dhamma. Some Buddhist schools and traditions have altered Shamatha-Vipassana meditation and some have even abandoned it for other techniques. The Buddha taught that any true and effective meditation practice must have two qualities: to quiet the mind and to gain insight. Shamatha-Vipassana meditation is a simple method with profound and transformative results. It is a method that anyone can integrate into their lives.

The purpose of shamatha-vipassana meditation is not to enter into a trance, or a mental state where thinking is distracted by an object or visualization. The purpose of shamatha-vipassana meditation is precisely what these words mean. To quiet the mind so that insight will arise. This meditation will bring a state of deep concentration and full awareness of the phenomenal world without being distracted by thoughts of clinging, craving, desire and aversion.

The Tibetan word for meditation is "gom" which means to become familiar with or to become intimate with. Shamatha-Vipassana meditation is the Buddha's meditation method for becoming familiar and intimate with your own mind.

Posture

There is nothing magical or mystical about a meditation posture. The typical meditation posture of being seated on the floor with legs folded against the torso is simply a way to sit comfortably during meditation. The meditation posture should be stable and relaxing and support a quiet and alert mind. It should provide a reasonable amount of comfort, avoiding physical distraction, for the meditation period. At first, any posture may prove to be uncomfortable, and the posture described below will become more comfortable with consistent practice.

Any pillows or cushions that are comfortable can be used. It is preferable to sit on the floor supported by a zafu (pillow made for meditation) placed over a zabuton (a larger, flatter mat to support the legs). The zafu should be from 6 to 8 inches thick and can be filled with cotton, buckwheat or kapok.

When sitting on the zafu (or pillow) place your sit bones on the front third of the zafu and allow your hips to naturally extend out in front of you. With your legs straight in front of you, bend your right leg at the knee and place your right foot under your left thigh and near your left buttock. Bend your left leg at the knee and place your left foot approximately in the crease formed by your right thigh and calf, resting on your calf. For additional support you can place yoga blocks or a rolled towel under your knees if needed.

This may be uncomfortable at first, but with time and patience this will prove to be a very stable base with which to build a meditation practice on. This is called the half-lotus or Burmese posture.

If you are particularly nimble, you may want to sit in the full-lotus position which is the same as the half-lotus with the exception of placing the right foot on top of the left thigh and the left foot on the right thigh. Again, there is nothing advantageous about the full-lotus over the half-lotus unless it affords you more stability and comfort.

From this stable base, keep your back straight but not stiff, not leaning forward or back. Align your ears with your shoulders and your nose with your navel. Place your left hand on top of your right palm with your thumb tips lightly touching, forming an approximate egg-shape with the thumbs and forefingers.

Again, there is nothing magical or mystical about this hand placement, it simply leads to relaxation and lessens physical distraction. If you are more comfortable with your hands palm down on your knees, or some other position, whatever provides the most comfortable and stable position is the meditation posture for you.

Consistency with your posture will allow your body and mind to recognize that meditation is taking place and your body and mind will begin to quiet as soon as the mediation posture is taken. A quiet body supports quieting your mind.

The Truth of Happiness Course

An alternative to sitting on a zafu is to use a low bench called a seiza in a sitting-kneeling position usually over a blanket or zabuton.

If sitting on the floor proves too uncomfortable, it is acceptable to sit in a chair with your feet flat on the floor, your back straight but not stiff, ears aligned with your shoulders and nose aligned with your navel.

Lying down is the least effective regular meditation posture as it will usually lead to drowsiness. If lying on your back is the only choice due to injury or illness, make the best of it and avoid drowsiness. If drowsiness ensues, stop meditation and begin again when refreshed.

The Shamatha-Vipassana Meditation

Technique

Shamatha-Vipassana meditation is a simple but profound method for developing a calm and well-concentrated mind. Avoid the ego-personality's need for constant stimulation and self-establishing

50

experiences and maintain the simplicity of the method.

Avoid bringing concepts unrelated to the dhamma into your meditation for "contemplation" or investigation. Avoid using meditation to develop attachments to objects or visions. Maintain the simplicity of the Buddha's meditation method and the results will be the same!

To begin your meditation, take a few slow, deep breaths, exhaling fully. Gently close your eyes and gently close your mouth, leaving a soft smile. Allow your body and mind to settle into your seat. Breathing through your nose, notice your breath entering your body at the tip of your nose. Being mindful of the sensation of breathing in your body you may notice that the air is slightly cooler on the inhale and slightly warmer on the exhale. If you don't notice this temperature difference simply notice the flow of your breath at the tip of the nose.

Be mindful of your inhalation and your exhalation. Do not attempt to regulate your breathing in any way. However your body wants to breathe, keep your mindfulness as best you can on the pure sensation of breathing.

Remember, you are not seeking a trance-like state or an avoidance of thinking. You are not attempting to develop a mind-state of "nothingness." While it is possible to set an intention to use meditation to manipulate a mind-state of nothingness. Nothingness is a mind-state similar to unconsciousness. This mind-state may even seem pleasant as it is an escape from what is occurring.

There is no useful development of insight into The Four Noble Truths or Impermanence, Not-Self, and Stress from a mind-state of nothingness, or similar mind-states. Useful and effective insight is developed with Shamatha-Vipassana meditation within the framework of the Eightfold Path.

The purpose of Shamatha-Vipassana meditation is primarily to develop concentration. Every time you find yourself caught up in your thinking and then return your mindfulness to your breath you are interrupting conditioned thinking and deepening concentration.

Give yourself a few moments to simply become aware of the sensation of breathing through the nose. Without placing any importance on thoughts, remain mindful of your breathing.

Thoughts will continue to flow, we are conscious beings.

With mindfulness of your breath thoughts will no longer be a distraction. With practice, you will develop samadhi, a non-distracted quality of mind.

Gently but with strong intention, place your mindfulness on the sensation of breathing. This is the beginning of developing great concentration and minimizing discursive, reactionary and distracting thinking.

As thoughts arise, gently put your thoughts aside, not following one thought with another thought, and place your awareness on your breathing. As thoughts arise, gently put your thoughts aside and remain mindful of your breathing. This is called being mindful of the breath, holding in mind your breathing.

If noticing the breath at the tip of your nose is difficult, simply remain mindful of the sensation of breathing. This is the basic and fundamental technique that the Buddha taught for shamatha, for quieting the mind as a preliminary, but integral, practice to vipassana, or insight.

It should be noted here again that the Buddha did not teach just shamatha or just vipassana. Both shamatha and vipassana are a part of a singular method of meditation. The Buddha taught that "meditation should lead to tranquility and insight."

In your day-to-day practice it is most effective to simply place your mindfulness on the sensation of breathing through the nose. Do not be concerned with interpreting whether a breath is long or short, shallow or deep, where it is felt most prominently, and do not try to alter the breath in any way. Simply begin meditation by putting aside thoughts as thoughts arise. Become mindful of the pure sensation of breathing. This simple and powerful method will quickly quiet the mind and bring calm abiding.

As your mind quiets and you are able to remain mindful of your breath for a few moments, dispassionately notice that you have feelings, emotional and/or physical. These feelings can be pleasant, unpleasant, painful or ecstatic. All feelings are simply to be acknowledged, recognized as impermanent, and put aside.

Through dispassionate mindfulness of whatever feelings arise in meditation and returning mindfulness to your breath you are interrupting discriminating, discursive and reactive conditioned thinking. Dispassionate mindfulness develops the ability to deepen concentration allowing for insight to arise.

You are beginning to train your mind to not be distracted by your own thoughts!

During meditation also take note of thoughts flowing. You are a conscious being and thoughts should be flowing. Wile it may seem peaceful, it is not conducive to developing concentration or insight when stuck in a trance-like mind state. Again, the purpose of this meditation is initially to not be distracted by your own thoughts.

When you find that you are caught up in your thoughts, with dispassionate mindfulness acknowledge that you are following one thought immediately with the next, and return your mindfulness to your breath. You are now creating spaciousness in your mind leading to deeper concentration and insight.

As your practice deepens you will become mindful of your perspective changing. You will develop a comprehensive view of your feelings and thoughts. You will be able to notice without reaction your own thought process and the intimate and clinging relationship between sensory contact, feelings, and discriminatory thoughts.

As your concentration deepens notice the impermanent nature of the quality of your mind.

You are developing the ability to stay mindfully present with whatever is arising without reaction while on your meditation cushion (or chair). This refined mindfulness will become more apparent off your cushion, too

Being mindful of your breath, feelings, thoughts and the quality of your own mind is known as the Four Foundations of Mindfulness. The lesson in week two will deepen your understanding of mindfulness in relation to the Dhamma.

At times when it seems to be difficult to quiet your mind, use the (slightly) more elaborate method of dispassionately noticing the length of your breath, noting that the in-breath is a short (or long) in-breath and the out-breath is short (or long). You can further dispassionately notice whether the breath is shallow or deep, tight or flowing, or whatever qualities seem appropriate. After a period of time, return to dispassionate mindfulness of your breath as it is.

As your mind returns to a tranquil state, dispassionately become mindful of persistent or recurring thoughts, thought constructs or physical sensations. As these arise, note them for a moment or

56

two. Acknowledge that these persistent thoughts and feelings are impermanent. Return your mindfulness to the pure sensation of breathing. This is the practice of shamatha-vipassana meditation.

What is this like? You are able to be mindful of the sensation of breathing in your body without becoming lost in the story playing out in your thoughts. You are not immediately following one thought with the next thought. There is some spaciousness in your mind and between thoughts. There is no reaction to your thoughts. Your mind is quiet and tranquil.

Gaining the quiet concentration that brings the ability notice the impermanence of feelings, thoughts, thought constructs, and mind states is significant. You are now engaging in the "vipassana" part of shamatha-vipassana meditation, gaining insight into the functioning of your own mind.

What is this insight? Simply that all feelings, thoughts, all experiences, are impermanent and empty of any lasting effect except for the effect caused by holding on to thoughts and thought constructs, which brings stress and unhappiness arising from clinging.

Your ego-personality is constantly seeking to establish itself in every object, view, or idea that occurs. This is conditioned thinking. Conditioned thinking is a clinging mind *conditioned* towards maintaining your ego-self.

By experiencing your thoughts while remaining tranquil, you are intentionally putting aside conditioned thinking. By remaining tranquil as thoughts arise, you are training your mind to accept the people and events of your life, including yourself, as they are.

This complete acceptance of thoughts as they are releases the grip that conditioned thinking has had on your thinking process, providing the means for ending conditioned thinking.

A subtle aspect of clinging is clinging to conditioned thoughts. The ego-self becomes so enamored with its self-referential, self-establishing thoughts that one can begin a kind of worship of thinking. If thinking is rooted in a wrong view of self and the world, no thinking rooted in wrong view can bring clarity and understanding.

Understanding wrong view and the need of the ego-self to establish and maintain itself in every thought that occurs will become more apparent as you develop the refined mindfulness that comes from shamatha-vipassana meditation.

For now it is enough to know that creating some spaciousness in your thinking, not following one thought immediately with the next, clinging one thought to another, you are diminishing your ego-self's hold on your thinking and your life.

The realization that it is the reaction caused by conditioned thinking that creates perception of any event now reveals the means for freedom and liberation from unhappiness. Let go of everything that arises. Cease attaching a discriminating (judgmental) thought to a thought and you will interrupt the discursive mental pattern of conditioned thinking.

As your shamatha-vipassana practice develops, the insight and spaciousness realized in sitting practice will become increasingly apparent in your life off your cushion. You will find that you are more peaceful and less reactive. This is an aspect of deepening concentration. You will find you are more present and mindful of life as life occurs.

The non-analytical insight, or vipassana, is what distinguishes the meditation taught by the Buddha from every other "meditation" technique.

Unless insight is developed, no freedom from conditioned thinking is possible. Until all conditioned thinking is recognized and put aside, it will prove impossible to escape the suffering caused by your own mind.

Once all conditioned thinking is recognized and put aside by engaging in Shamatha-Vipassana meditation, and integrating the other seven factors of the Eightfold Path, the conditions necessary for awakening are established.

If unpleasant thoughts arise, put them aside and return to the sensation of breathing in your body. If pleasant thoughts arise, put them aside and return to the sensation of breathing in your body. If visions arise, pleasant or unpleasant, grand or mundane, dispassionately put them aside and return to the sensation of breathing in your body.

Whatever arises during meditation practice is simply part of what is to be recognized as impermanent and put aside, and return mindfulness to your breath. Remaining dispassionate with all mind states that arise during meditation begins to develop the ability to remain dispassionate throughout life, whether meditating or involved in mundane activities.

At the end of each meditation session take a moment to notice the quality of your mind. This is integrating the Fourth Foundation of Mindfulness into your meditation practice. Is your mind tranquil or agitated or distracted?

Dispassionately note the present quality of your mind. Be at peace with the quality of your mind in the present moment and you will immediately begin developing an understanding of impermanence and how your feelings and thoughts impact the quality of your mind.

Eventually remaining dispassionately mindful leads to the development of equanimity, a mind free of reaction, completely at peace and fully as life occurs. Equanimity is the free and natural state of an un-conditioned mind.

Establishing a Meditation Practice

Perhaps the most difficult challenge when beginning a meditation practice, and often as your practice develops, is organizing your life for practice. The busy-ness and nearly constant distractions of life are always creating the illusion that you are just too busy to practice. The irony is that meditators often find that they have more time for the most important activities of their lives when they do make the time for meditation practice. Committing to meditation twice a day and, within reason, keeping to this schedule is itself part of practice.

The most skillful time to practice is when you think you don't want to or think you don't have the time to sit. Every time you meditate you are diminishing the effects of conditioned thinking, including the conditioned thinking of aversion to practice.

As stated previously, meditating upon arising in the morning is usually the most effective time to schedule a first meditation session. If possible, meditating approximately 12 hours later in the day will provide a skillful balance to practice. If the only other time for practice is just before bed, be mindful of drowsiness, and if it is at times difficult to maintain alertness, try to adjust your schedule to earlier in the evening.

If it is possible to set aside a room solely for meditation, keep the room clean and clutter free. The room should also be well ventilated and seasonally not too hot or cold. A candle to light during meditation and perhaps a small statue of the Buddha as a mindful reminder of a human being who awakened can be an initial point of focus, but are not necessary.

If it is not possible to designate an entire room to your practice, a corner of a room that can be maintained as above will work just as well.

Developing a routine of place, time, posture and technique will greatly enhance your commitment to practice and help subdue your conditioned mind's desire to avoid the peaceful and enlightening refuge of a true and effective meditation practice.

It is most effective to begin a meditation practice with just a few minutes of meditation at a time. By initially meditating for two or three minutes at a time, twice a day, you will not become disappointed or conclude that meditation is too difficult. As you become comfortable with two or three minutes of practice, gradually add a minute or two to your meditation time. Stay at this length of meditation practice until you are comfortable and feel it is time to lengthen your meditation practice again.

If you have an established meditation practice using a different method, please use the meditation method described herein for the duration of the course. If you are meditating for longer periods than a few minutes, but only once a day, it will be most effective to split your meditation practice into two sessions without increasing your overall meditation time.

If taking the correspondence course please note the length of your meditation sessions in your weekly email.

Meditation practice is not an endurance test and should not create more stress by having too high expectations of yourself and your practice. The strongest impediment to establishing a meditation practice will prove to be your own judgments of yourself and your practice.

As you progress over the next nine weeks, gradually increase your meditation sessions to ten to twenty minutes. On occasion you may want to meditate for even longer periods. Take your time and remember that what is most important is a consistent practice that is free of grasping.

It is most skillful not to push yourself too hard and too fast, and also to not avoid increasing your length of meditation practice time when appropriate.

Establishing a meditation practice will be much more effective if done daily for short periods of time rather than long periods of meditation only occasionally.

Joining a regular meditation group that stays focused within the framework of The Eightfold Path is a great support to Dhamma practice.

If you are following the instructions, putting aside thoughts as they arise, not following a thought with a thought as best as you can, and returning your awareness to the sensation of breathing in your body, you are establishing a meditation practice.

Avoid judging yourself or your practice harshly. Always be loving and gentle with yourself and enjoy your practice.

This Week's Dhamma Study

- Listen to the week one talk on Shamatha-Vipassana meditation: http://crossrivermeditation.com/truth-of-happiness-online-course-talks/

- Begin to establish your meditation practice with a few minutes of meditation upon arising and again approximately 12 hours later in the day.

- Notice any persistent thoughts or feelings and your awareness of the impermanence of all thoughts. Avoid being analytical. This is a dispassionate observance of thoughts and feelings as they arise and pass away.

- Continue your Dhamma study with week two.

- Always be gentle with yourself and enjoy your practice!

If taking the correspondence course:

- At the end of your first week write a paragraph or two regarding your Dhamma practice and write down any questions or insights you have.

- To submit your writing, please use this form: http://crossrivermeditation.com/home-study-submissions/

- I will respond to you within 24 to 48 hours.

Wk 1

⟶ Who was the Buddha?
⟶ What is this going about what will we learn about?
⟶ Why are these teachings
⟶ how? - general
— foci
- Pali cannon
— today

66

Week Two
The Four Foundations
of Mindfulness

"Friends, this is the only way for the purification of beings, for the overcoming of sorrow and lamentation, for the destruction of suffering and grief, for reaching the right path, for the attainment of Nibbana, namely, the Four Foundations of Mindfulness." [4]

In the Satipatthana Sutta the Buddha teaches the Four Foundations of Mindfulness. A practice of mindfulness without this foundation can often lead to confusion and distraction on the path of liberation and freedom. Right Mindfulness is the seventh factor of The Eightfold Path. It is part of a practice of transcending stress and unhappiness, rather than simply reducing or managing stress.

Mindfulness used to manage the stress of modern life in the phenomenal world can and does bring great benefit to human health. Mindfulness with the intention to manage or reduce stress does not have the same intention, known as Right Intention or Right Resolve, as what the Buddha taught. Holding in mind Right Intention will provide ongoing guidance for your meditation practice.

Right Intention is explained in week four.

The Four Foundations of Mindfulness is taught to bring immediate mindfulness of what is occurring during shamatha-vipassana meditation. Mindfulness is the quality of mind that supports developing lasting peace and happiness. Practicing mindfulness within the context of The Four Noble Truths is straightforward, accessible, easily understood and practiced. The Four Foundations of Mindfulness are:

1. Being mindful of the breath in the body
2. Being mindful of feelings arising from the six-sense base. (explained below)

3. Being mindful of thoughts arising from the six-sense base.

4. Being mindful of the present quality of mind (explained below)

The six-sense base is your five physical senses and conscious thought. It is through the six-sense base that self-referential contact and self-identification (attachment) with phenomenon is established. The six-sense base is explained in additional detail in week eight.

The first foundation of mindfulness, being mindful of the breath in the body, is the same mindfulness practiced in shamatha-vipassana meditation. In shamatha-vipassana meditation, you begin to quiet your mind by putting aside thoughts as thoughts arise and becoming mindful of your breathing, preferably the sensation of breathing through the nose.

You are using mindfulness of your breath in the body to cease being distracted by your thoughts and to begin developing concentration. This is the essence of mindfulness. Mind in a distracted state is focused outside the physical body. You must understand where your mind is focused in order to free yourself of a mind distracted by clinging, craving, aversion, and discursive and compulsive thinking.

Being mindful of what is occurring in relation to The Eightfold Path through holding in mind your breath in the body is the foundation of developing understanding of your ego-personality and its relation to the distraction of stress.

Being mindful of your breath in your body interrupts outer-focused clinging conditioned thinking and begins to quiet your mind with directed inner mindfulness.

The second foundation of mindfulness, being mindful of feelings, becomes possible once your mind has quieted enough to be able to hold in mind your breath in you body for a few moments. Once a tranquil mind state has been achieved and mindfulness of the breath is maintained, notice any feelings, emotional or physical, that arise. If you become mindful of an emotion such as frustration, anger, fear, resentment, etcetera, simply recognize that a feeling has arisen, and, while maintaining mindfulness of your breath, put aside any thoughts in reference to the feeling.

You may want to begin to blame yourself or others to justify the feeling. Put these thoughts aside.

You may be drawn to analyze the feeling in some other way. You may ask yourself where did the feeling come from, what circumstances took place to bring a rise to the feeling? Put these thoughts aside. It is enough to recognize the feeling for what it is while maintaining mindfulness of your breath.

With mindfulness of your breath let go of the feeling. Let go of the judgment attached to the feeling. Judging a feeling creates clinging and develops emotion. An emotion is a reaction to an event, judging an event in some way. The reaction caused by judgment further intensifies the feeling and further conditions your conditioned mind.

Notice that it is a reaction to an external event that was perceived through one or more of your six senses that initiated the feeling. It is at the point of contact with the external experience that a personal, self-referential, attachment is made. By developing mindfulness of this process you will gain insight and understanding of the subtle but pervasive and continual establishment of a self that is prone to confusion and suffering. This is the ongoing process of "I-making" also known as conceit.

Recognition of the initiation of I-making develops the ability to bring continued I-making to cessation.

Mindfulness is a dispassionate focused awareness on whatever is arising in the present moment without being distracted by any judgments or discriminating thoughts. Being mindful of feelings as feelings arise allows the feeling to dissipate and allows a deeper tranquility to develop.

If a physical sensation arises such as pain or discomfort in some area of your body, remain mindful of the sensation of breathing. Note the physical sensation and the immediate self-identification, and return your mindfulness to your breath. Again, do not judge the physical sensation in any way. Do not wish that you are not having the experience of discomfort or agitation. Simply note the experience while maintaining mindfulness of your breath.

Being mindful of physical sensations without further judgment often will minimize the sensation. Returning your mindfulness to your breath interrupts your reaction to physical and emotional feelings.

This is the second foundation of mindfulness: being mindful that through contact with your five physical senses and consciousness, feelings arise. Being mindful of feelings, being ardent and aware of feelings as feelings arise, begins to de-condition conditioned mind by interrupting the discursive and self-perpetuating judgment and analysis of feelings.

Simply and dispassionately be mindful of feelings as feelings arise while maintaining mindfulness of the breath.

The third foundation of mindfulness is being mindful of your thinking process. With dispassionate mindfulness notice how your thoughts evaluate impermanent qualities of your mind. Notice if your mind is agitated or peaceful. Notice if your mind is constricted or spacious. Dispassionately notice your thoughts attached to the quality of your mind, often driven by feelings. This begins to develop insight into how your thoughts have created confusion and suffering. With insight you can begin to incline your mind towards release from clinging conditioned mind.

Remember that shamatha-vipassana meditation is primarily used to develop unwavering concentration. This entire process of noting feelings and thoughts is done with dispassionate mindfulness. Feelings arise that take your attention. Note that a feeling has your attention and return your mindfulness to your breathing. When you find that you are distracted by discriminating thoughts related to the changing quality of your mind simply note the quality of your mind and return your mindfulness to your breath.

Mindfulness is holding in mind. Being mindful that thoughts are flowing develops your innate ability to control thoughts. Being mindful of thoughts is recognizing that thinking is taking place. Unless concentration is developed, thoughts tend to feed themselves from conditioned thought patterns. This is discursive thinking and is an aspect of clinging mind.

Through refined mindfulness it becomes clear that thoughts are an ongoing judgment of feelings and mental states. Much mental energy and distraction is spent on recollecting harsh or extreme judgments. This is a form of mindfulness. This type of unrefined mindfulness can be debilitating. If left unchecked this can lead to ever intensifying emotions that can result in depression and anxiety, or other mental disease.

The type of refined mindfulness developed in this course is knowing what to hold in mind and in what context.

Being mindful of thoughts without attachment, dispassionately remaining ardent and aware of thinking while maintaining mindfulness of the breath in the body will interrupt discursive thinking, allowing your mind to quiet and allowing your mind to remain at peace. As mindfulness and concentration develops, the afflictions caused by discursive thinking subside and a mind of equanimity, a non-reactive mind, is maintained.

The fourth foundation of mindfulness is being mindful of the present (but impermanent) quality of your mind. Is your present quality of mind inclined towards craving, clinging, and the continuation of stress? Is your present quality of mind inclined towards developing wisdom and release from craving and clinging?

This is a broader type of mindfulness that notices the quality of your mind that has developed from defining yourself through self-referential experiences driven by feelings and conditioned thinking. Notice when your mind seeks further sensual stimulation. Notice when your mind is distracted by ill-will. Notice when your mind is dull or restless or anxious or distracted by uncertainty.

This is developing mindfulness of The Five Hindrances. The Five Hindrances are explained in week ten.

Remember that this is a dispassionate "noticing" that develops an understanding of your clinging conditioned mind. When any of these qualities are noted return your mindfulness to your breath.

As concentration deepens and mindfulness broadens notice the development of the qualities of Right Effort, Right Mindfulness, Right Concentration, serenity, and equanimity.

Right Effort, Right Mindfulness, and Right Concentration are three factors of the Eightfold Path. The Eightfold Path is explained beginning in week four.

The Four Foundations of Mindfulness is also known as "The Four Frames of Reference." You are developing mindfulness (and concentration) in the context of the Four Noble Truths.

What this means is that as you continue to develop concentration and mindfulness you begin to integrate the Four Noble Truths more deeply into your life. You will begin to understand stress and how the quality of your mind is either inclined towards continuing stress or developing release from craving, clinging and the cessation of stress.

Through a true practice of mindfulness within the framework of The Eightfold Path, you gain the ability to understand that the state of your mind, the mental quality of your mind in the present moment is dependent on, and caused by, your previous mind-states. At first simply being mindful of whatever quality your mind is experiencing is enough. As mindfulness of breath, feeling, and thought develops, and understanding and awareness of the quality of mind develops, you gain the ability to put away greed & distress with reference to the world. This is called Right Mindfulness.

With Right Mindfulness you gain an understanding of mind as the vehicle of perception. Right Mindfulness is recognizing and abandoning craving and clinging arising from ignorance. Having put aside all afflictions, this is the mind of equanimity, a mind fully engaged in the phenomenal world without discriminating or discursive thinking, a mind completely free of reaction.

As noted previously, Right Mindfulness is the seventh factor of The Eightfold Path and directly precedes the teaching on Right Meditation in order to emphasize the necessity to develop right mindfulness. Right Mindfulness is the foundation for an authentic and effective meditation practice, all within the Right Understanding of The Four Noble Truths.

Mindfulness truly is the foundation of all of the teachings of the Buddha. By practicing mindfulness within the context of The Four Noble Truths, you can free yourself of the stress and suffering caused by mindlessness. Mindfulness within the context of The Four Noble Truths will develop an awakened mind, a mind of pure equanimity.

Right Mindfulness is reviewed in relation to The Eightfold Path in week six. It is included here so that you can begin to develop mindfulness together with your meditation practice.

The Buddha concluded his teaching on The Four Foundations of (Right) Mindfulness with a promise: "'This is the direct path for the purification of beings, for the overcoming of sorrow & lamentation, for the disappearance of pain & distress, for the attainment of the right method, & for the realization of Unbinding — in other words, the four frames of reference.' Thus was it said, and in reference to this was it said." [5]

This Week's Dhamma Study

- Listen to the week two talk on the Four Foundations of Mindfulness: http://crossrivermeditation.com/truth-of-happiness-online-course-talks/

- Continue with your meditation practice in the morning and early evening.

- In meditation, remain mindful of your breathing as you dispassionately notice feelings and thoughts arise and dissipate. Become aware of your mind from a dispassionate observational view, a mind-state of choiceless awareness, always mindful of your breath. Choiceless awareness is a non-discriminating mind state. Thoughts that arise in meditation are not judged or analyzed in any manner. Thoughts are simply observed with dispassionate awareness.

- Notice any persistent thoughts and your awareness of the impermanence of all thoughts. Avoid being analytical. This is a dispassionate observance of thoughts and feelings as they arise and pass away.

- Always be gentle with yourself and enjoy your practice!

- Continue your Dhamma study with week three.

If taking the correspondence course:

- At the end of your second week write a paragraph or two regarding your Dhamma practice and write down any questions or insights into the Four Foundations of Mindfulness.

- To submit your writing, please use this form: http://crossrivermeditation.com/home-study-submissions/

- I will respond to you within 24 to 48 hours.

Week Three
The Four Noble Truths

At the Buddha's very first teaching when he presented The Four Noble Truths to the five wandering ascetics he had previously befriended on their search for enlightenment, he described awakening in very simple an direct terms:

"Vision arose, discernment arose, insight arose, knowledge arose within me of things never heard of before: The truth of dukkha (stress) has been comprehended; the origination of stress has been abandoned; the cessation of stress has been experienced; The Eightfold Path leading to the cessation of stress has been developed." [6]

As will be stated a few times in this course, awakening is dependent on acquiring a few specific skills so that these four tasks can be accomplished. There are three skills needed that are developed in this course.

- Shamatha-Vipassana meditation is used to develop unwavering concentration known as Samadhi.

- A useful and refined quality of mindfulness is developed to allow for insight into the true nature of human existence.

- Deep and profound wisdom is developed to see clearly craving and clinging arising from an ego-personality and to maintain fee of the world's entanglements.

Also, all eight factors of the Eightfold Path can be seen as tasks to be accomplished for the successful completion of the path and for developing a life of lasting peace and happiness. The skills of heightened concentration, refined mindfulness and wisdom are all necessary skills to develop in order to fully integrate the Eightfold Path.

Everything the Buddha taught for the final forty-five years of his life, after his awakening, was taught in the context of the Four Noble Truths.

I will again identify these tasks individually following the description of each noble truth.

This week you will develop a deeper understanding of The Four Noble Truths. This understanding is the foundation for a lifetime of developing lasting peace and happiness through a practice of heightened wisdom, heightened virtue, and heightened concentration.

Notice the word foundation. Every teaching the Buddha presented rests on the foundation of The Four Noble Truths. Once this foundation is in place the continued integration of these truths into your life will lead to profound changes in how your life is experienced.

This training is straightforward and basic and easily understood by anyone who applies the teachings and develops understanding through continued practice.

You will also begin to develop an understanding of mindfulness within the context of The Four Noble Truths.

Many people come to a meditation or mindfulness practice believing that a meditation or mindfulness technique alone will be sufficient to relieve the causes of all unhappiness and stress. It is true that any technique that brings one's mind and body to a state of stillness and developed mindfulness will have positive physical and mental benefits.

The purpose and intent of this course is not for stress reduction, although as progress is made, stress is reduced. The purpose and intent of this course, and the teachings this course is based on, is the ending of stress and unhappiness. In order to develop the ending of stress and unhappiness, meditation and mindfulness must be developed within a broader framework than only ordinary meditation or mindfulness techniques. This framework is called "The Eightfold Path" or "The Eight-Factored Path" as there are eight factors to this training.

A reminder about terminology: The word that the Buddha used to describe unhappiness and stress is Dukkha. Dukkha also can be translated to mean unsatisfactoriness, disappointment, disillusionment, disenchantment, suffering and confusion. The belief in a permanent ego-personality, or an ego-self, is also dukkha as it is an ego-self that is prone to ongoing confusion and suffering. The Buddha used the word "Anatta" which means "not-self" to indicate that what is commonly viewed as a self is not a self worth establishing and defending. I will use the words unhappiness and stress interchangeably to signify all manifestations of Dukkha. I will use the words ego-self, ego-personality, not-self, and anatta interchangeably.

First we will look a little deeper at The Four Noble Truths from the perspective of understanding, as understanding is the foundation of this course:

The Four Noble Truths can be defined as a statement of conditions, or a statement of the truth of these conditions:

1. Life is stressful

2. Clinging and craving cause stress

3. Cessation of stress is possible

4. The Eightfold Path develops the cessation of
    stress

Through developing understanding using refined mindfulness and shamatha-vipassana meditation, within the framework of the Eightfold Path, knowledge of the truth of these conditions becomes apparent:

The First Noble Truth

The Truth of Stress and Unhappiness

Stress occurs impersonally to all. As a consequence of birth we are all subject to physical phenomena which no one, regardless of social position, intellect, religious or spiritual understanding, or "grace," can avoid. We are all subject to sickness, aging and eventually death. Along the way we will all face loss, some minor, some quite devastating. According to our environment we will acquire views of how we should live our lives, who we want to associate with, what we would like to achieve, and an endless list of likes and dislikes.

All of these experiences and the resulting discriminating thoughts contribute in a cumulative manner to stress. We all know that every experience is subject to change. Impermanence and uncertainty are a part of life. Underlying this knowing is a subtle tension.

We know that certain activities may bring disappointment or sickness. We may not feel secure financially and fear of personal physical loss will be present. Whatever our position in life might be, we create attachments to our lives being a certain way. These are different for everyone but the result is the same. These attachments form a self-referential identity, or ego-personality.

This is clinging, or more specifically clinging the ego-self to objects, events, views. and ideas that serve to describe and define (and severely limit) what is commonly and wrongly viewed as a person.

Stress arises in our lives the instant we want the people and events of our lives to be different than they are. Due to the impermanence of all things, wanting the people and events of our lives to remain as they are also brings stress. This includes ourselves and our view of our selves.

Do you want more of a certain experience? Do you want less of a certain experience? Are you always looking for something new to avoid facing a general disappointment with life? Does fear of change occupy your thoughts? Does fear that change won't occur occupy your thoughts? Is boredom, the need for constant distraction, motivating your thoughts and actions? This list is endless and all of these thoughts produce stress and distract from life as life is occurring.

Boredom is a common problem when beginning to establish a meditation practice. Boredom is the need for continual distraction and will subside as concentration increases.

Even pleasurable experiences generate stress as the positive feeling will develop craving. Craving develops from the insatiable need for sensory fulfillment of your ego-personality. Primarily, craving is due to the defining characteristic of life: impermanence. All things in life are subject to impermanence. You only need to take a dispassionate look at yourself to begin to see and understand impermanence. As soon as you are born you begin to age. Putting aside the benefits or drawbacks to aging, you age.

Simply as a consequence of living you move towards death moment by moment. Along the way it is certain that there will be physical difficulties living in and maintaining your body. There are likely to be mental and emotional difficulties as well. Becoming mindful of life's impermanence removes the uncertainty that leads to stress. Understanding that all things are impermanent ends clinging and craving.

Lao Tzu, the Chinese sage and writer of the Tao Te Ching stated: "Once you understand the impermanence of all things, you will hold onto nothing."

When you have an experience that brings pleasure you want to hold onto the pleasure-giving experience. Attachment (clinging) to the event conditions your mind to desire similar experiences. Impermanence intervenes, change is inevitable, stress arises.

Unpleasantness and disappointment brings the same response. An unpleasant experience arises, a change from a pleasant (or neutral) quality of mind occurs, and due to clinging to the pleasant (or neutral) quality of mind, stress arises. Change does not occur quick enough and additional stress arises. Aversion to the unpleasant event conditions your mind and stress arises. Aversion is a form of clinging through the desire that an event (or object, view, or idea) be different than what has occurred.

Position, power, wealth, intellect, ignorance, the right religion, philosophy, or spiritual discipline, none of these will insulate one from stress.

Continuously seeking what brings pleasure and attempting to avoid that which is unpleasant, is to be constantly grasping after the impermanent and transitory.

By continuously grasping after satiating the ego-personality through achievements and acquisitions, including intellectual achievements, is to be constantly grasping after the impermanent and transitory.

We have seen that inherent in life there will be difficulties, disappointments and unhappiness. All things in life change and all human beings are prone to sickness, aging and eventually death. Along the way, events will arise that will bring great pleasure and great disappointment.

It is within this impermanent environment that you live your life and stress arises. It is also within this impermanent environment that stress and unhappiness can be understood. Once understood, craving and clinging, the causes of stress, can be abandoned.

A life of freedom and true happiness is possible for anyone. All that is required to gain freedom from stress is to understand integrate four truths, beginning with the truth of stress.

Before we look at the origin of stress, let's look at who, or what, is experiencing stress.

We have seen that the environment that stress arises in is impermanent and ever-changing. We have identified the pervasiveness of stress within that environment. What is it that is subject to stress? What is it that causes stress to arise? What is it that can bring an end to stress?

Of course the answer is you (and all human beings.) You are the cause of your stress due to clinging, craving, desire and aversion. You can also bring the end to stress in your life. Only you can. First you must understand what it is that constitutes this thing called "I,' "me," or "self."

What is commonly viewed as a self is nothing more than a personality prone to craving, clinging, and suffering. This view was acquired through experiencing the events of life from an ignorant view.

This is not to be seen as being ignorant in a general sense. The ignorance referred to here is ignorance of The Four Noble Truths.

This wrong view is further influenced by the impermanent environment of the phenomenal world and the associations developed. This personality is typically identified as the "ego."

(Not-self or non-self is the term most often used in Buddhist terminology to signify the ego-self or ego-personality. The Buddha used the term Anatta, which means not-self or non-self, to signify the impermanence and insubstantiality of the ego-personality that is perceived as self. The common view of self is a wrong view when arising from ignorance. Not-self or non-self is not meant to imply no self or nothingness.)

Your ego-personality is as impermanent as any other aspect of the environment of which it is a part. In fact, through insight gained through shamatha-vipassana meditation, your ego-personality will be seen as a constantly changing creation of your own views.

It is helpful to begin to objectify your ego-personality. This will help diminish clinging to views of self.

Not understanding the impermanence of your ego-personality and how your ego-self creates an identity by clinging to objects, views, and ideas is ultimately the cause of all stress. Understanding this ongoing process brings the end to stress, disenchantment and unhappiness.

We have now defined three key points of this course:

1. The impermanence of all things, including your view of yourself.

2. The pervasiveness and unavoidable nature of stress.

3. The ego-self as an impermanent personality arising from ignorance and formed by experiences, environment, and associations.

These are known as "The Three Linked Characteristics of Existence," or "The Three Marks of Existence." In the original Pali language they are Anicca, Dukkha and Anatta or Impermanence, Stress and Not-Self. We will look deeper at these three characteristics of existence in week seven.

For now it is enough to know that it is a lack of knowledge, or ignorance, of who you are, and an aversion to acknowledge the environment that you exist in, that continues stress and unhappiness.

Wisdom is gaining an understanding of the interaction of impermanence, stress, and the ego-personality.

Wisdom is taking a realistic look at who you are and the choices and attachments you make.

Wisdom is recognizing unskillful choices and unskillful attachments to objects, ideas, and views that have arisen from ignorance.

Wisdom is making mindful choices and conclusions based on the true nature of existence.

Wisdom is understanding developed through the Eightfold Path.

"The truth of dukkha (stress) has been comprehended." The task associated with the First Noble Truth is to fully comprehend stress (Dukkha).

Ignorance is insisting that the personality viewed as I or me is permanent and well-established. Ignorance is continually reacting to life based on what makes this ego-personality satisfied. This is simply "feeding the ego." Feeding what cannot be satisfied is a constant distraction and only grows your ego-self.

The problem of conditioned thinking maintaining your ego-self becomes much more complex as your ego-personality develops. The originating cause is simple:

The Second Noble Truth

The Truth of the Origination of Stress

Clinging, craving, desire and aversion originate stress. Wanting the people and events of your life to be different then they are is craving or desire. Attachment to the people and events of your life to remain as they are is clinging. Clinging arises from ignorance and defines you through continued clinging that binds you to this limiting conditioned view - who you think you are is all you think you are.

Due to the initial wrong view of yourself, you believe that your personality is all that you are. As a consequence of this wrong view of self, you have developed a constant need to defend and satiate your ego-personality.

Letting go of clinging does not mean that you won't have physical and emotional needs met. Letting go of clinging means letting of your need to have your ego-personality's needs met. Letting go of clinging means letting go of the mental preoccupation arising from the attachments to the people and events of your life. Letting go of clinging is also letting go of all views arising from ignorance.

95

Through shamatha-vipassana meditation within the framework of The Eightfold Path you will gain insight into your ego-personality and the choices and attachments you make arising from wrong view. You will begin to realize that sensory-driven impulses animate much of what you do. You will see how clinging and craving are ego-personality based.

Most importantly you will learn to see your ego-personality realistically and not spend your life driven by sensory fulfillment and the need to continually establish and defend your ego-personality.

It is through gaining a realistic view of self, a Right View, and the choices made based on Right View that you can begin to put all stress and unhappiness aside. You won't be able to gain a realistic and clear view of self if you continue to remain distracted by your own ego-personality and its constant need for attention.

This constant attention is the distraction caused by stress. A mind that is constantly distracted by the sensual needs of an ego-personality will never be free and at peace. A mind that has gained the ability to not be distracted by its own sensory-driven needs and desires is a mind free of stress. A mind free of stress is a mind of lasting peace and happiness.

"The origination of stress has been abandoned." The task associated with the Second Noble Truth is to abandon craving and clinging.

The Third Noble Truth

The Truth of the Cessation of Stress

As we have seen, the cause of stress is craving and clinging in all their forms arising from a misunderstanding of who you are and the nature of your environment. Experiencing the cessation of stress and unhappiness requires letting go of clinging, craving, desire and aversion. Abandoning clinging and craving becomes possible once the true nature of anatta, your ego-self, is understood. As you integrate the teachings of this course, an understanding of the futility of clinging to any object, view, or idea in the environment of impermanence is understood.

It is important to remember that it is within the environment of impermanence (anicca) that stress arises and it is also in the environment of

97

impermanence that unhappiness and stress ends. Impermanence gives rise to clinging but impermanence also allows for the cessation of suffering. If the nature of all phenomenon were not impermanent, cessation of stress would not be possible.

We have identified the problem as stress (dukkha). We have identified the cause of the problem as craving and clinging. The path that brings the ability to recognizing and abandon craving and clinging and experience the cessation of suffering is the Eightfold Path.

The Eightfold Path is the framework for developing heightened virtue and heightened concentration leading to the development of heightened wisdom.

Developing these three qualities brings an end to craving and clinging. It is your ego-personality's need to continually establish, satisfy and proliferate itself that leads to non-virtuous actions.

It is your ego-self, that which the Buddha teaches is anatta, not a self, that insists on establishing itself in every object, view, and idea that occurs. To a deluded (un-awakened) mind all objects, views, and ideas are self-referential.

As you begin to interrupt the thought-reaction pattern that clinging and craving cause, your mind begins to quiet. At first this is very subtle. Heightened wisdom, heightened virtue and heightened concentration increases with every non-reactive, non-craving, non-self-referential thought or action. This begins to diminish the hold of your ego-personality's reactive mind.

Shamatha-Vipassana meditation begins to quiet your mind enough to allow for recognition of clinging, craving, desire and aversion. As meditation practice develops, concentration increases. As your mind is less distracted by your own craving thoughts, you will cease clinging onto and grasping after all that is impermanent. Eventually you will gain true wisdom and realize the impermanence of your own ego-personality. You will cease clinging to all impermanent objects, views, and ideas.

"The cessation of stress has been experienced." The task associated with the Third Noble Truth is to experience the cessation of stress.

The Fourth Noble Truth
The Truth of the Path Leading to the
Cessation of Dukkha

We will develop deeper understanding of The Eightfold Path beginning with next week's class. A brief introduction will suffice for now. As stated, The Eightfold Path is a framework for developing heightened wisdom, heightened virtue and heightened concentration. The first two factors of The Eightfold Path are the wisdom factors. The next three factors are virtuous factors. The final three are the concentration factors.

The wording should not be taken in a strict moral sense. Rather, the wording describes that there are definite right views and actions to take that will prove effective in achieving the end of stress. The implication is that there are also wrong views and actions, and unskillful applications of mindfulness and concentration, that if not recognized and abandoned will continue confusion, stress and unhappiness.

Referring to The Eightfold Path as a framework for Dhamma practice is a reminder to be mindful of all thoughts, words and deeds in relation to this path. The Eightfold Path is what you are to be mindful of if you are to succeed in eliminating the effects of stress on your life.

The Eightfold Path

1. Right View
2. Right Intention
3. Right Speech
4. Right Action
5. Right Livelihood
6. Right Effort
7. Right Mindfulness
8. Right Meditation

"The Eightfold Path leading to the cessation of stress has been developed." The task associated with the Fourth Noble Truth is to develop the path leading to the cessation of stress.

Next week we will begin to develop a deeper understanding of The Eightfold Path and how to live your life within this framework.

This Week's Dhamma Study

- Listen to the week three talk on The Four Noble Truths:
  http://crossrivermeditation.com/truth-of-happiness-online-course-talks/

- Continue with your meditation practice in the morning and early evening. Add a minute or two to your meditation sessions if you are comfortable with the length of your meditation sessions.

- In meditation, remain mindful of your breathing as you dispassionately notice feelings and thoughts arise and dissipate. Become aware of your mind from a dispassionate observational view, a mind-state of choiceless awareness always mindful of your breath.

- Begin to take note of the impermanence of all things and in particular your own thoughts.

- Notice any persistent thoughts and your awareness of the impermanence of all thoughts. Avoid being analytical. This is a dispassionate observance of thoughts and feelings as they arise and pass away.

- Continue your Dhamma study with week four.

- Always be gentle with yourself and enjoy your practice!

If taking the correspondence course:

- At the end of your third week write a paragraph or two regarding your Dhamma practice and your developing understanding of The Four Noble Truths. Are you gaining an understanding of how clinging, craving, desire and aversion create stress and unhappiness? Do you understand that cessation of stress and unhappiness is possible to achieve through The Eightfold Path? Write down any questions or insights into your practice, the nature of impermanence, and how clinging and craving create unhappiness and stress. Note how long you are meditating.

- To submit your writing, please use this form: http://crossrivermeditation.com/home-study-submissions/

- I will respond to you within 24 to 48 hours.

Week Four
The Eightfold Path
Right View and Right Intention

Heightened Wisdom

"It is for the full comprehension, clear understanding, ending and abandonment of suffering that the Noble Eightfold Path is to be cultivated." [7]

The Eightfold Path is the path to be developed leading to lasting peace and happiness. It is the fourth of The Four Noble Truths. The Eightfold Path is the framework for Dhamma practice. All eight factors are to be integrated into the life of a practitioner of the Dhamma. Each factor contributes to a cohesive system of developing insight and understanding of impermanence and the distraction of stress.

The Eightfold Path is a path of Heightened Wisdom, Heightened Virtue and Heightened Concentration.

The first two factors contribute to the development of Heightened Wisdom:

1. Right View

2. Right Intention

There are three factors that develop Heightened Virtue:

1. Right Speech

2. Right Action

3. Right Livelihood

Three additional factors contribute to the development of Heightened Concentration:

1. Right Effort

2. Right Mindfulness

3. Right Meditation

Right View is both an entry point into the Dhamma and, with practice, the state of mindful presence free of the distraction of stress.

As you begin to integrate the Eightfold Path into your life, and diminish the views and actions arising from your ego-self, your moment-to-moment life becomes an expression of an awakening human being.

Keep in mind the stated purpose of the Dhamma is understanding the origination of stress and experiencing the cessation of stress. Being mindful of this singular purpose will be a great benefit in recognizing otherwise wholesome activities that are a distraction from developing understanding.

I will separate these eight factors into the three natural divisions of The Eightfold Path. While it is wisdom that develops and deepens as understanding develops and deepens, Right View also provides the initial perspective for Dhamma practice and Right Intention provides initial direction.

Right View and Right Intention

The Wisdom Factors

The purpose of practicing The Eightfold Path is to experience the cessation of the distraction of stress. Stress describes the ongoing mental/physical states experienced by your ego-self in the phenomenal world. Stress ranges in experience from general unsatisfactoriness and disappointment to extreme emotional and physical suffering.

A reminder about terminology: The word that the Buddha used to describe unhappiness and stress is Dukkha. Dukkha also can be translated to mean unsatisfactoriness, disappointment, disillusionment, disenchantment, suffering and confusion. I will use the words unhappiness and stress interchangeably to signify all manifestations of Dukkha.

Ignorance, lacking wisdom, as to the truth of human existence gives rise to the distraction of stress.

The Four Noble Truths provide an understanding of ignorance and the pervasiveness of the distraction of stress. Clinging and craving is shown to be the origination of the distraction of stress. The Third Noble Truth shows that cessation of stress can be developed. The Fourth Noble Truth is the truth of the path leading to the cessation of unhappiness and stress, The Eightfold Path.

Right View

The first factor or component of The Eightfold Path is Right View. Right View implies wrong view. Wrong view is a view of yourself and the world that is ignorant of The Four Noble Truths. This course and the Buddha's teachings are to develop Right View and complete knowledge and understanding of The Four Noble Truths.

Right View is initially the perspective that your views of life have been lacking understanding, lacking wisdom. This lack of wisdom has given rise to craving and clinging leading to unhappiness and stress. Stress is a distracted mind state born of ignorance. Preoccupation with stress is the distraction that keeps one in ignorance.

Remember, this is not stating that you, or all human beings are generally ignorant, only that ignorance of The Four Noble Truths leads to suffering.

Understanding that it is your own ignorance of The Four Noble Truths that has caused your distracted mind state of stress is acknowledging the truth of stress. Remember that the task associated with The First Noble Truth is a complete understanding of stress. Right View then is understanding stress in the context of The Four Noble Truths.

The skills required to accomplish the task of understanding stress are heightened concentration, useful insight, and refined mindfulness. The skills are developed within the framework of the Eightfold Path.

Without the initial perspective that wisdom and understanding in the context of The Four Noble Truths is lacking, it will be impossible to develop the understanding leading to the cessation of stress. Acknowledging that it is your own lack of wisdom that has caused disillusionment and suffering can be difficult at first.

Until this initial step is taken your mind will reject developing understanding. Your mind will remain wandering around in ignorance looking for any distraction to avoid seeing the truth.

Without the perspective of Right View, developing the path of liberation would be like planning a trip to Los Angeles when you are departing from New York but believing and insisting that you are in Chicago.

It is impossible to arrive at your destination, lasting happiness and peace, without first acknowledging your present quality of mind. Achieving liberation and freedom from stress cannot be realized without first accepting the truth of stress and its causes.

Ultimately Right View is the perspective of a mind resting in the Dhamma free of the distraction of stress, an awakened mind. Right View develops gradually. Initially an understanding that life in the phenomenal world is stressful and the cause of stress is clinging begins the development of wisdom. Through integrating all eight factors of The Eightfold Path, Right View develops understanding that penetrates to the root of suffering.

Developing Right View is developing wisdom. The Buddha describes Right View:

"And what is right view? Knowledge with regard to stress, knowledge with regard to the origination of stress, knowledge with regard to the cessation of stress, knowledge with regard to the path or practice that develops the cessation of stress: This is called right view." [8]

Right View is knowledge and understanding of The Four Noble Truths. Right View is a view that supports developing concentration and wisdom.

Right View is considered the forerunner of the path:

"And how is right view the forerunner? One discerns wrong view as wrong view, and right view as right view. This is one's right view. And what is wrong view? There is nothing given, nothing offered, nothing sacrificed. There is no fruit or result of good or bad actions. There is no this world, no next world, no mother, no father, no spontaneously reborn beings; no Brahmans or contemplatives who, faring rightly & practicing rightly, proclaim this world & the next after having directly known & realized it for themselves." [9]

The Buddha here is describing the ignorance and the consequences of wrong view: "There is nothing given, nothing offered, nothing sacrificed" means that clinging, craving, desire and aversion to objects, views, and ideas are maintained, not given (up).

"There is no fruit or result of good or bad actions" means that there is no understanding of the consequences of delusion.

"There is no this world, no next world, no mother, no father, no spontaneously reborn beings; no Brahmans or contemplatives who, faring rightly &

practicing rightly, proclaim this world & the next after having directly known & realized it for themselves" refers to lacking understanding of the process of becoming, kamma, or rebirth.

Wrong view is the view that compels one to phenomenal (worldly) attainment, acquisition, and attachment.

Initially wrong view is simply recognized. As Right View is developed, actions originating in wrong view are abandoned. It is wrong view that continues to develop kamma and it is wrong view that, due to kamma, causes rebirth. Wrong view is caused by ignorance, Right View is an expression of wisdom.

Kamma and Rebirth are explained in detail in week nine.

The Buddha explains how Right Effort and Right Mindfulness directly contribute to developing wisdom:

"One tries to abandon wrong view & to enter into right view: This is one's right effort. One is mindful to abandon wrong view & to enter & remain in right view: This is one's right mindfulness. Thus these three qualities - right view, right effort, & right mindfulness - run & circle around right view." [10]

Right View supports and informs all of the components of The Eightfold Path. Having engaged with The Four Noble Truths, Right View brings wisdom to a mind previously stuck in ignorance and confusion.

The consequences of wrong view(s):

"In a person of wrong view, wrong resolve (wrong intention) comes into being. In a person of wrong resolve, wrong speech. In a person of wrong speech, wrong action. In a person of wrong action, wrong livelihood. In a person of wrong livelihood, wrong effort. In a person of wrong effort, wrong mindfulness. In a person of wrong mindfulness, wrong concentration. In a person of wrong concentration, wrong knowledge. In a person of wrong knowledge, wrong release.

"This is how from wrongness comes failure, not success." [11]

Holding wrong views founded in ignorance can never lead to Right View, wisdom, and liberation. All views born of ignorance are wrong views and are to be recognized and abandoned.

"**Be mindful of wrong view and enter and remain in Right View.**" [12] *This is the task associated with Right View.*

Right Intention

Right Intention is having the intention to abandon all views and abandon all that would continue ignorance and stress. Right Intention is the intention to abandon all clinging and craving.

Right Intention is also included as the second factor of The Eightfold Path as it leads directly to the development of the virtuous factors of Right Speech, Right Action and Right Livelihood. Along with the intention to abandon clinging and craving, Right Intention is also the intention to abandon ill-will and all harmful thoughts, words and deeds.

Right View initially brings a recognition of wrong views. Due to strong mental fabrications, or conditioned thinking, that have developed from wrong view, recognition alone is not enough to gain liberation and freedom from stress.

Right Intention, holding the firm intention to abandon craving and clinging and develop the experience of the cessation of suffering, strengthens

Right View. Right Intention can be seen as an expression of Right View. The entire transformative nature of the Dhamma arises from Right Intention.

Being mindful of Right Intention brings clarity to the destructiveness of reactive thoughts, words and deeds caused by ignorance.

Without Right Intention the virtuous and concentration factors of the Path cannot be developed. The ego-self has too much invested in wrong views to put all wrong views aside without the strong resolve of Right Intention. The impermanent ego-personality will not yield if wrong views are not abandoned and Right Views developed. Holding the intention to abandon all wrong views naturally brings the mind to the virtuous and concentration factors of the path. (Reviewed in weeks five and six)

Holding the intention to abandon all clinging and craving and to abandon all ill-will and harmful thoughts, words and deeds begins to diminish the effects that occur as a result of a strong attachment to your ego-self. Right View is also called Right Thinking and Right Perspective.

It is wrong thinking that binds impermanent views to a temporary ego-personality. It is wrong thinking that develops craving from a temporary ego-personality. Clinging and craving arise from a misunderstanding of what a self is and how a self has arisen. Misunderstanding the nature of self develops an ego-personality that suffers in ignorance from birth, sickness, aging, death and rebirth.

It is this personality that the Buddha identified as "anatta." Anatta means "not-self" or "non-self." This is often misunderstood to imply that awakening is the extinguishing of being. Awakening is the extinguishing of an insubstantial, impermanent personality that has arisen from wrong views. It is this personality that is subject to the distraction, confusion and suffering of stress.

Impermanence, Dukkha and Not-Self is explained in detail in week seven.

Right Intention is the intention to abandon all views of an impermanent self so that Right View may be developed completely.

Impermanence describes the environment in which ignorance and stress (dukkha) arise. Impermanence also describes the environment that a "self" develops ignorance resulting in the distraction of stress.

A wrong view of self develops behavior that manifests in non-virtuous ways. If it were not for a confused mind subject to stress and strongly committed to maintain its existence, there would be no need for a path of liberation.

As stated previously, once the wisdom of The Four Noble Truths has entered a mind suffering in ignorance, that same mind can now hold the Right Intention to awaken. Your ego-personality's strong resistance to letting go of wrong views can only be overcome by the foundation developed initially by Right View and Right Intention. Right View is your entry to Dhamma practice and Right Intention sets and holds your direction.

Initial Right View acknowledges The Four Noble Truths to be true.

Right Intention is the holding the intention to engage whole-heartedly with the Eightfold Path and recognize and abandon craving and clinging.

"Be mindful of wrong intention and enter and remain in Right Intention." [13] *This is the task associated with Right Intention.*

Next week's class will show how Right Speech, Action and Livelihood logically follow Right View and Intention. With the support of the other factors of The Eightfold Path, Right Speech, Action and

Livelihood lead directly to the experience of the cessation of unhappiness and stress.

This Week's Dhamma Study

- Listen to the week four talk on Right View and Right Intention: http://crossrivermeditation.com/truth-of-happiness-online-course-talks/

- Continue with your meditation practice in the morning and early evening. If you feel comfortable with adding a few minutes to your practice do so. 5 to 10 minutes for each session should be comfortable now.

- In meditation, remain mindful of your breathing as you dispassionately notice feelings and thoughts arise and dissipate. When you notice that you are caught up in your own thoughts and have lost awareness of your breath, put aside the focus on your thoughts and place your awareness on your breathing. Become aware of your mind from a dispassionate observational view, a mind-state of choiceless awareness always mindful of your breath.

- Continue to develop wisdom by noticing your attachments to the people and events of your life, including your views of self. Begin to generate the Right Intention to let go of all attachments and all impermanent views.

- Notice any persistent thoughts and your awareness of the impermanence of all thoughts. Avoid being analytical. Shamatha-Vipassana meditation practice is a dispassionate observance of thoughts and feelings as they arise and pass away. Take note of your developing wisdom and your own resolve to develop lasting peace and happiness.

- Continue your Dhamma study with week five.

- Always be gentle with yourself and enjoy your practice!

If taking the correspondence course:

- At the end of your fourth week write a paragraph or two regarding your Dhamma practice and your developing understanding of The Four

Noble Truths. Explain your understanding of Right View and Right Intention as the initial factors of The Eightfold Path. Explain how being mindful of Right View and Right Intention will support development of the experience of the cessation of the distraction of Dukkha. Note how long you are meditating.

- To submit your writing, please use this form: http://crossrivermeditation.com/home-study-submissions/

- I will respond to you within 24 to 48 hours.

Week Five
The Eightfold Path
Right Speech, Right Action,
Right Livelihood

Heightened Virtue

— how do I incline my mind T towards it?

"When the mind is inclined towards the
Dhamma, the disciple of the noble ones gains a sense
of the goal, gains a sense of the Dhamma, gains joy
connected with the Dhamma. In one who is joyful,
rapture arises. In one who is rapturous, the body
grows calm. One whose body is calmed experiences
ease. In one at ease, the mind becomes concentrated."
[14]

Right View initially is being mindful of The
Four Noble Truths beginning with the truth of stress.

Clinging, craving, desire and aversion all cause unhappiness and stress. Right View then brings to mind the possibility of the cessation of stress. Understanding the cause of the distraction of stress, and the possibility to end stress, Right View develops mindfulness of the Path leading to the cessation of stress.

Being Mindful of Right View, Right Intention develops the presence of mind and the strong resolve to abandon craving and clinging. It is craving for or clinging to any object or view that perpetuates unhappiness and stress. It is clinging to all objects, views, and ideas that have arisen from ignorance that must be recognized and abandoned.

Mindfulness as presented in The Eightfold Path is developing mindfulness of all views of an impermanent ego-personality. It is craving for objects, views and ideas that support the establishment of an ego personality that initiates clinging. As understanding develops it becomes clear that preoccupation with views attached to an ego-self maintains stress. Once this process is recognized, and craving and clinging diminish, preoccupation and distraction lessens. As distraction lessens Samadhi, non-distraction increases. The practical benefits of the Eightfold Path begin to become apparent.

It is the preoccupation with stress that creates the distraction that continues wrong views. It is ignorance that gives rise to the belief that your ego-personality is who you are and all that you are. Having this limited and wrong view of yourself gives rise to grasping, aversion and delusion.

Out of this mental/physical aggregation an individual personality arises. It is this personality that makes choices and takes action based on attachment and perceived needs. The base need of the ego-personality is to continue to define and maintain the ego-self and its beliefs in all objects, views and ideas.

The mental/physical aggregation known as The Five Clinging-Aggregates is explained in week eight.

Mindfulness of Right Speech, Right Action, and Right Livelihood, the three virtuous factors of The Eightfold Path, shows clearly where attachments to an ego-personality have formed. The ego-self or ego-personality is consciousness influenced by physical senses and interpreting the sensory stimulation from the perspective of clinging conditioned mind.

This is why meditation alone cannot bring lasting peace and happiness. Without a framework grounded in Right View, meditation can reinforce craving, clinging, and hurtful views arising from an ego-self. Due to the nature of conditioned mind, the entire framework of The Eightfold Path is necessary to develop concentration, insight, and wisdom.

The Buddha taught: "A true and effective Dhamma practice must incorporate these three trainings. Which three? The training in heightened virtue, the training in heightened concentration, the training in heightened discernment (wisdom)." [15]

Right Speech is the third factor of The Eightfold Path. By mindfully integrating Right Speech it becomes clear how words are used to continue establishing a self that is prone to stress.

Right Speech:

- Abstaining from lying, speaking truthfully

- Abstaining from divisive speech, including gossip, speaking with compassion for all

- Abstaining from abusive speech, speaking with kindness and tolerance

- Abstaining from idle chatter, speaking only what is necessary and helpful

Wrong speech arises from clinging, craving and aversion. It is often used to promote or defend the ego-personality. Wrong Speech can be very subtle at times. Gossip in particular is always hurtful and always arises from the desire to promote an ego-personality. It is best to only speak of others when they are present.

Idle chatter is used as much for distraction as for social interaction. Kalyanmitta means spiritual friendship. True friendships are friendships that are maintained without idle chatter. As wisdom develops, an understanding that spoken words will actually be helpful to someone or a situation will also show if they are necessary. Words that have no meaningful impact are part of idle chatter and can often prove divisive and will always be distracting.

Right Speech also pertains to what you are saying to yourself and should be considered within the same guidelines. Is your self-talk truthful, helpful, kind and compassionate? Are your thoughts a type of unnecessary idle chatter?

From the perspective of Right View and the direction provided by Right Intention, Right Speech develops to very subtle levels. Once gross wrong speech is identified and mindfully abandoned, recognition of speech that may have seemed helpful and altruistic may now be seen to be manipulative and designed to elicit a particular response or reaffirm an ego-personality, yours or other's.

Being mindful of words expressed towards others will show the state of your well-being and understanding. Being mindful of self-talk will deepen understanding of craving and clinging. and the further establishment of your ego-self.

"Be mindful of wrong speech and enter and remain in Right Speech." [16] *This is the task associated with Right Speech.*

Right Action and Right Livelihood follow the same moral, ethical and practical guidelines as Right Speech.

Right Action:

- Abstaining from taking life, remaining harmless to all beings

- Abstaining from taking what is not freely given, taking only what is offered

126

- Abstaining from sexual misconduct, acting with generosity and kindness

- Abstaining from selfish acts, Acting for the good of all

As with Right Speech, mindfulness of your actions will show your attachments and what you most closely identify with. Kamma means action and it is the unfolding of intentional actions moderated by mindfulness that determines the direction and overall experience of your life. (Kamma and Rebirth are explained in week nine.)

"Be mindful of wrong action and enter and remain in Right Action." [17] *This is the task associated with Right Action.*

Right Livelihood:

- Abstaining from dishonesty, profiting from virtuous acts ⊃ positive impact

- Abstaining from hurtful endeavors, contributing to the common good

- Abstaining from the sale of intoxicants

- Abstaining from the sale of weapons or harmful items

Right Livelihood is remaining harmless when earning a living while contributing to the common good. While many of us do not have a direct choice for our livelihood, the product of our efforts should fall within these guidelines.

"Be mindful of wrong livelihood and enter and remain in Right Livelihood." [18] *This is the task associated with Right Livelihood.*

It requires great wisdom coupled with compassion to know when to speak and take action, and when to practice restraint. Compassion without wisdom can often be hurtful. It is often less than skillful to speak or act solely to make others feel better about themselves or to further validate other's wrong views. Throughout the Pali canon the Buddha presented the example of restraint of speech when speaking would only reinforce someone's wrong views.

As virtue is developed, an understanding of the importance of bringing wisdom to compassionate thoughts, words and deeds develops. In the Ratana Sutta, the discourse on the Three Jewels, the Buddha and his attending monks first addressed the physical and emotional needs of a town that had been devastated by natural occurrences and disease. They then presented the Dhamma in a way that would have meaning.

An article on the Ratana Sutta is included at the end of this book.

The Ratana Sutta also shows that Dhamma practice is not effective as an isolated event practiced only on our cushions or "special" occasions or special situations. In order to develop virtue, concentration and wisdom, Dhamma practice is engaged in mindfully moment by mindful moment.

By maintaining mindfulness of your thoughts, words, and deeds without defense, deep insight into conditioned thinking arises. This is the practical mindfulness and insight that is necessary in order to abandon all aspects of the distraction of stress and to awaken.

Right Speech, Right Action, and Right Livelihood are grounded in Right View and Right Intention and are supported by Right Effort, Right Mindfulness, and Right Meditation.

This Week's Dhamma Study

- Listen to the week five talk on Right Speech, Action and Livelihood:
  http://crossrivermeditation.com/truth-of-happiness-online-course-talks/

- Continue with your meditation practice in the morning and early evening. If you feel comfortable with adding a few minutes to your practice do so. 5 to 10 minutes of meditation each session should be comfortable now.

- In meditation, remain mindful of your breathing as you dispassionately notice feelings and thoughts arise and dissipate. When you notice that you are caught up in your own thoughts and have lost awareness of your breath, put aside the focus on your thoughts and place your awareness on your breathing. Continue your awareness of your mind from a dispassionate observational view, a mind-state of choiceless awareness, mindful of your breath.

- Continue to develop wisdom by noticing your attachments to the people and events of your life, including yourself. Continue to generate the Right Intention to let go of all attachments and all impermanent views.

- In your day-to-day life notice when you are engaged in Right Speech, Action and Livelihood and when you are not. Develop the strong intention to abandon all wrong speech, action and livelihood. As concentration deepens, non-virtuous thoughts, words and deeds become apparent.

- Notice any persistent thoughts and your awareness of the impermanence of all thoughts. Avoid being analytical. This is a dispassionate observance of thoughts and feelings as they arise and pass away. Take note of your developing wisdom and your own resolve to develop lasting peace and happiness.

- Continue your Dhamma study with week six.

- Always be gentle with yourself and enjoy your practice!

If taking the correspondence course:

- Write a paragraph or two regarding your Dhamma practice and write down any questions or insights into incorporating Right Speech, Right Action and Right Livelihood into your life and how developing Heightened Virtue will contribute to the experience of the cessation of stress and unhappiness.

- To submit your writing, please use this form: http://crossrivermeditation.com/home-study-submissions/

- Send me an email to schedule a phone or online video chat instruction session. Please request a few half-hour time periods on Thursdays between 10 am and 8:30 pm, Fridays between 10 am and 8:30 pm, Saturdays between 11 am and 2:30 pm or Sundays between 10 am and 1 pm. These are Eastern Times. John@CrossRiverMeditation.com

- I will respond to you within 24 to 48 hours.

Week Six
The Eightfold Path
Right Effort, Right
Mindfulness,
Right Meditation

Heightened Concentration

"There are the four developments of concentration. There is the development of concentration that leads to a pleasant abiding in the here & now. There is the development of concentration that leads to the attainment of knowledge & vision. There is the development of concentration that leads to mindfulness & alertness.

There is the development of concentration that leads to unbinding and the cessation of suffering." [19]

The Eightfold Path is the Buddha's framework for developing understanding leading to the cessation of stress. It is a path that develops heightened wisdom, heightened virtue and heightened concentration, or heightened Samadhi.

Samadhi is a quality of mind of non-distraction. Shamatha-Vipassana meditation within the framework of The Eightfold Path develops non-distraction from the effects of clinging, craving, desire and aversion.

I will use concentration to describe Samadhi.

Heightened wisdom is developed within the framework of The Eightfold Path with Right View and Right Intention. Initially, mundane wisdom inspires the mind to understand the validity and authenticity of The Four Noble Truths. This is a turning point in the ongoing distraction of unhappiness and stress.

A mind that has developed the mundane understanding that its view has been confused and distracted by its own clinging and craving can now develop wisdom and Right View. This same mind can now begin the process of abandoning all causes of confusion and distraction, all causes of stress and unhappiness.

From Right View, Right Intention develops. Right Intention is being mindful of abandoning all causes of stress. Being mindful of the intention to abandon craving and clinging leads to the development of the virtuous factors of the path.

Being mindful of, and abandoning, all that is not Right Speech, Right Action and Right Livelihood, develops useful mindfulness of craving and clinging. Being mindful to maintain Right Speech, Right Action and Right Livelihood develops the ability to diminish and finally abandon craving and clinging.

Your thoughts and resulting actions, when mindfully observed, provide clear insight into the your current state of understanding.

As your thoughts, words, and deeds become more peaceful your mind is naturally more peaceful.

As clinging begins to diminish, a practice of developing heightened concentration becomes effective. Right Effort is the first of the three factors of heightened concentration.

Right Effort

Right Effort is generating the skillful desire, actions, and diligence to:

- Avoid inappropriate thoughts, words and deeds that have yet arisen.

- Abandon inappropriate thoughts, words and deeds that have arisen.

- Develop appropriate thoughts, words and deeds that have yet arisen.

- Maintain appropriate thoughts, words and deeds for continual development of non-confusion and skillful qualities that have arisen. [20]

Right Effort emphasizes the importance of abandoning non-virtuous acts. Being mindful of Right Effort brings understanding that it is by strong attachment to the ego-personality that non-virtuous acts occur. As current non-virtuous behavior is abandoned, virtuous behavior can be further developed. Through mindful awareness of what is to be developed and what is to be abandoned, appropriate thoughts, words and deeds are now the foundation for continued Right Effort.

This is a refined application of mindfulness that is developed and maintained in the Dhamma. Being mindful of what is to be abandoned and what is to be developed is the essence of Right Mindfulness.

Right Effort is one factor (of eight) in developing the path of liberation and freedom from the confusion and distraction of stress. It is part of a cohesive method of understanding The Four Noble Truths. Dhamma practice begins at the point of accepting the First Noble Truth, the Truth of Unhappiness and Stress.

From this initial Right View, acceptance of the necessity to change ego-centered views becomes apparent.

Right Intention follows to bring to mind the resistance to changing views that conditioned thinking maintains. It takes mindful determination to overcome the effects of the confusion and distraction that your ego-personality has developed.

Right Effort will develop the qualities needed for liberation from stress and unhappiness. Engaging in Dhamma practice should not lead to harsh judgments on past behavior.

With the perspective of Right View, Right Effort is an intentional change in the way your thoughts, words and deeds affect your development of understanding. Right Effort is the mindful turning point from conditioned reaction to the people and events of your life to being mindfully and dispassionately present with what is occurring. Right Effort develops a mindful and skillful presence arising from developing wisdom.

A mindful and dispassionate quality of mind is not aloof disengagement from the people and events of life. Dispassionate mindfulness is being fully present with whatever arises without discriminating thoughts of craving, clinging, avoidance, or aversion.

The Eightfold Path is not a sequential training, beginning at Right View and ending at Right Meditation. The foundation of understanding begins with Right View and progresses through the next seven factors. As understanding develops, all eight factors of the path are integrated into your life as a cohesive Dhamma practice.

Right Effort also refers to the practical development of the remaining two concentration factors of the path.

Right Effort is developing a deeper understanding of the teachings of the Buddha. The implication here is that wrong effort is being distracted by activities or teachings that create confusion and further the establishment of ego-centered views.

You are engaged in Right Effort in your study of the Dhamma. Right Effort is the mindful effort to develop the entire Eightfold Path.

"One efforts to abandon wrong view, wrong intention, wrong speech, wrong, action, wrong livelihood, wrong mindfulness and wrong meditation and develop Right View, Right Intention, Right Speech, Right Action, Right Livelihood, Right Mindfulness, and Right Meditation. This is one's Right Effort." [21]

Right Effort also refers to organizing one's life for Dhamma practice. Organizing time for meditation practice and quiet time is Right Effort. Engaging in a meditation practice that develops tranquility and insight is Right Effort. Right Effort is being a supportive member of a sangha that maintains focus on The Four Noble Truths, if possible. Right Effort is effort spent understanding and developing The Four Noble Truths.

Developing the path leading to the cessation of dukkha is Right Effort.

The Buddha describes Right Effort succinctly:

"Abandon what is unskillful (craving and clinging) and develop what is skillful (The Eightfold Path). If it were not possible to abandon what is unskillful and develop what is skillful, I would not teach this. If it were harmful to abandon what is unskillful and develop what is skillful, I would not teach this. Apply your efforts to develop what is skillful." [22]

"Be mindful of wrong effort and enter and remain in Right Effort." [23] *This is the task associated with Right Effort.*

Right Mindfulness

The focus of your thoughts will determine experience. Thoughts preoccupied with clinging, craving and aversion will lead to more confusion and stress. Thoughts well-concentrated on mindfulness of the Dhamma will bring lasting peace and happiness.

Distracted thoughts focused on fleeting desires, achievements, and acquisitions can only lead ⅄ to more confusion and stress. Thoughts and actions that create additional self-identities, even altruistic self-identities, can only lead to more confusion and stress. Thoughts that establish and reinforce the ego-personality in any manner, in any realm ,can only lead to more distraction, confusion and stress.

This includes the modern "Buddhist" concepts of an inner Buddha-nature, achieving Buddhahood, or rituals and practices engaged in with the intention for more favorable experiences and rebirths.

These are concepts introduced in the later-developed Buddhist religions that adapted the Buddha's teachings to accommodate individual and cultural influences. Often, continued establishment of the ego-self, continued I-making, is the result of these accommodations.

Mindfulness in the context of The Four Noble Truths is to abandon the distraction of stress arising from craving clinging, and remain focused on The Eightfold Path. Mindfulness of the entire Eightfold Path develops understanding that will end the confusion and suffering born of ignorance of The Four Noble Truths.

Many useful applications of mindfulness have been developed. Some applications of mindfulness techniques have greatly enhanced the health field in dealing with pain and stress. There is no need to abandon any mindfulness technique for specific health issues as long as they do not reinforce your ego-personality.

It is not skillful to equate the mindfulness of the Dhamma with modern applications of mindfulness. The generally stated purpose of modern mindfulness techniques is to manage mental and physical pain, and stress. Mindfulness techniques when applied in this context are often successful in achieving this purpose.

The mindfulness of the Dhamma is to develop understanding of The Four Noble Truths and the complete cessation of stress.

Mindfulness is to recollect or to hold in mind.

- Be mindful to abandon wrong view and enter and remain in Right View

- Be mindful to abandon wrong intention and enter and remain in Right Intention

- Be mindful to abandon wrong speech and enter and remain in Right Speech

- Be mindful to abandon wrong action and enter and remain in Right Action

- Be mindful to abandon wrong livelihood and enter and remain in Right Livelihood

- Be Mindful to abandon wrong effort and enter and remain in Right Effort

- Be mindful to abandon wrong mindfulness and enter and remain in Right Mindfulness

- Be Mindful to abandon wrong meditation and enter and remain in Right Meditation [24]

These are the tasks associated with Right Mindfulness.

The refined mindfulness that is so effective in developing the entire Eightfold Path is simply to remain mindful of the Eightfold Path as your life unfolds, moment by moment.

Holding in mind the Eightfold Path is bringing the framework of the Eightfold Path into your life. As the path becomes integrated into your life, your life becomes an expression of heightened wisdom, heightened virtue, and heightened concentration.

The result of your Right Effort is a life of lasting peace and happiness.

The following section on mindfulness was presented in week two. It is presented again here to bring mindfulness into the context of the entire Eightfold Path.

In the Satipatthana Sutta the Buddha teaches the Four Foundations of Mindfulness. A practice of mindfulness without this foundation can often lead to confusion and distraction. Right Mindfulness is the seventh factor of The Eightfold Path. It is part of a practice of ending stress and unhappiness, rather than simply reducing or managing stress.

Mindfulness used to manage the stress of modern life in the phenomenal world can and does bring great benefit to human health. Mindfulness with the intention to manage or reduce stress does not have the same intention, known as Right Intention or Right Resolve, as what the Buddha taught. Holding in mind Right Intention determines the ensuing result of any action or activity.

Right Intention was explained in week four.

The Four Foundations of Mindfulness is taught to bring immediate mindfulness of what is occurring during shamatha-vipassana meditation without distraction. Mindfulness is the quality of mind that supports developing lasting peace and happiness. Practicing mindfulness within the framework of The Four Noble Truths is straightforward, accessible and easily understood and practiced. The Four Foundations of Mindfulness are:

1. Being mindful of the breath in the body

2. Being mindful of feelings arising from the six-sense base. (explained below)

3. Being mindful of thoughts arising from the six-sense base.

4. Being mindful of the present quality of mind (explained below)

The six-sense base is your five physical senses and conscious thought. It is through the six-sense base that self-referential contact and self-identification (attachment) with phenomenon is established. The six-sense base is explained in additional detail in week eight.

The first foundation of mindfulness, being mindful of the breath in the body, is the mindfulness of the breath practiced in shamatha-vipassana meditation. In shamatha-vipassana meditation, you begin to quiet your mind by putting aside thoughts as thoughts arise while becoming mindful of your breathing, preferably the sensation of breathing through the nose.

You are using mindfulness of your breath in the body to cease being distracted by your thoughts and to begin developing concentration. This is the essence of mindfulness. Mind in a distracted state is focused outside the physical body. You must understand where your mind is focused in order to free yourself of a mind distracted by clinging, craving, aversion, and discursive and compulsive thinking.

Being mindful of what is occurring in relation to The Eightfold Path through holding in mind your breath in the body is the foundation of developing understanding of The Four Noble Truths.

Being mindful of your breath in your body interrupts outer-focused clinging conditioned thinking and begins to quiet your mind with directed inner mindfulness.

The second foundation of mindfulness, being mindful of feelings, becomes possible once your mind has quieted enough to be able to hold in mind your breath in you body for a few moments. Once a tranquil mind state has been achieved and mindfulness of the breath is maintained, notice any feelings, emotional or physical, that arise. If you become mindful of an emotion such as frustration, anger, fear, resentment, etcetera, simply recognize that a feeling has arisen, and, while maintaining mindfulness of your breath, put aside any thoughts in reference to the feeling.

147

You may want to begin to blame yourself or others to justify the feeling. Put these thoughts aside. You may be drawn to analyze the feeling in some other way. You may ask yourself where did the feeling come from, what circumstances took place to bring a rise to the feeling? Put these thoughts aside. It is enough to recognize the feeling for what it is while maintaining mindfulness of your breath. With mindfulness of your breath let go of the feeling. Let go of the judgment attached to the emotion.

An emotion is a reaction to an event, judging an event in some way. The reaction caused by judgment further intensifies the feeling and further conditions your conditioned mind.

Notice that it is a reaction to an external event that was perceived through one or more of your six senses that initiated the feeling. It is at the point of contact with the external experience that a personal, self-referential, attachment is made. By developing mindfulness of this process you will gain insight and understanding of the subtle but pervasive and continual establishment of a self that is prone to confusion and suffering. This is the ongoing process of "I-making" also known as conceit.

Recognition of the initiation of I-making develops the ability to bring continued I-making to cessation.

Mindfulness is a dispassionate focused awareness on whatever is arising in the present moment without being distracted by any judgments or discriminating thoughts. Being mindful of feelings as feelings arise allows the feeling to dissipate and allows a deeper tranquility to develop.

If a physical sensation arises such as pain or discomfort in some area of your body, remain mindful of the sensation of breathing. Note the physical sensation and the immediate self-identification. Again, do not judge the physical sensation in any way. Do not wish that you are not having the experience of discomfort. Simply note the experience while maintaining mindfulness of your breath.

Being mindful of physical sensations without further judgment often will minimize the sensation. Returning your mindfulness to your breath interrupts your reaction to physical and emotional feelings.

This is the second foundation of mindfulness: being mindful that through the five physical senses and consciousness, feelings arise within. Being mindful of feelings, being ardent and aware of feelings as feelings arise, begins to de-condition conditioned mind by interrupting the discursive and self-perpetuating judgment and analysis of feelings.

Simply and dispassionately be mindful of feelings as feelings arise while maintaining mindfulness of the breath.

The third foundation of mindfulness is being mindful of your thinking process. With dispassionate mindfulness notice how your thoughts evaluate impermanent qualities of your mind. Notice if your mind is agitated or peaceful. Notice if your mind is constricted or spacious. Dispassionately notice your thoughts attached to the quality of your mind, often driven by feelings. This begins to develop insight into how your thoughts have created confusion and suffering. With insight you can begin to incline your mind towards release from clinging conditioned mind.

Remember that shamatha-vipassana meditation is primarily used to develop unwavering concentration. This entire process of noting feelings and thoughts is done with dispassionate mindfulness. Feelings arise that take your attention. Note that a feeling has your attention and return your mindfulness to your breathing. When you find that you are distracted by discriminating thoughts related to the changing quality of your mind simply note the quality of your mind and return your mindfulness to your breath.

Notice the impermanence of thoughts. Notice the impermanence of feelings. Notice the interplay of feelings and thoughts and how feelings influence thoughts, and vice-versa. Notice your (diminishing) preoccupation with impermanent feelings and thoughts.

Mindfulness is holding in mind. Being mindful that thoughts are flowing develops your innate ability to control thoughts. Being mindful of thoughts is recognizing that thinking is taking place. Unless concentration is developed, thoughts tend to feed themselves from conditioned thought patterns. This is discursive thinking and is an aspect of clinging mind.

Through mindful awareness it becomes clear that thoughts are an ongoing judgment of feelings x and mental states. Left unchecked this can lead to ever intensifying emotions that can result in depression and anxiety, or other mental disease.

Being mindful of thoughts without attachment, dispassionately remaining ardent and aware of thinking while maintaining mindfulness of the breath in the body will interrupt discursive thinking, allowing your mind to quiet and allowing your mind to remain at peace. As mindfulness and concentration develops, the afflictions caused by discursive thinking subside and a mind of equanimity, a non-reactive mind, is maintained.

As your understanding and integration of the Eightfold Path deepens, you will begin to see the relationship of your thoughts and resulting actions in the context of the Eightfold Path. This is a dispassionate and non-analytical observance of how your thoughts and actions are inclined towards the skillful, or "right" aspects of the Eightfold Path and will lead to liberation, or are inclined towards further confusion and disappointment.

The fourth foundation of mindfulness is being mindful of the present (but impermanent) quality of your mind. Is your present quality of mind inclined towards craving, clinging, and the continuation of stress? Is your present quality of mind inclined towards developing wisdom and release from craving and clinging?

This is a broader type of mindfulness that notices the quality of your mind that has developed from defining yourself through self-referential experiences driven by feelings and conditioned thinking. Notice when your mind seeks further sensual stimulation. Notice when your mind is distracted by ill-will. Notice when your mind is dull or restless or anxious or distracted by uncertainty.

Notice when your mind is resistant, or averse, to what is occurring, including the present quality of your mind. Notice how this aversion creates reaction which develops further agitation. This is mindlessness, losing control of your mind from reaction to temporary mind states.

This is developing mindfulness of The Five Hindrances. The Five Hindrances are explained in week ten.

Remember that this is a dispassionate "noticing" that develops an understanding of your clinging conditioned mind. When any of these qualities are noted return your mindfulness to your breath.

As concentration deepens and Right Mindfulness broadens notice the development of the qualities of Right Effort, Right Mindfulness, Right Concentration, serenity, and equanimity.

The Four Foundations of Mindfulness is also known as "The Four Frames of Reference." You are developing mindfulness (and concentration) in the context of the Four Noble Truths.

What this means is that as you continue to develop concentration and mindfulness you begin to integrate the Four Noble Truths more deeply into your life. You will begin to understand stress and how the quality of your mind is either inclined towards continuing stress or developing release from craving, clinging and the cessation of stress.

Through a true practice of mindfulness within the framework of The Eightfold Path, you gain the ability to understand that the state of your mind, the mental quality of your mind in the present moment is dependent on, and caused by, your previous mind-states.

At first simply being mindful of whatever quality your mind is experiencing is enough. As mindfulness of breath, feeling, and thought develops, and understanding and awareness of the quality of mind develops, you gain the ability to put away greed & distress with reference to the world. This is called Right Mindfulness.

With Right Mindfulness you gain an understanding of your mind as the vehicle of perception. Perception is a view of worldly occurrences and your relationship to the world that is either formed by ignorance, or informed by knowledge, of The Four Noble Truths.

Right Mindfulness is recognizing and abandoning craving and clinging arising from ignorance. Having put aside all afflictions, this is the mind of equanimity, a mind fully engaged in the phenomenal world without discriminating or discursive thinking, a mind free of reaction.

As noted previously, Right Mindfulness is the seventh factor of The Eightfold Path and directly precedes the teaching on Right Meditation in order to emphasize the necessity to develop right mindfulness. Right Mindfulness is the foundation for an authentic and effective meditation practice, all within the Right Understanding of The Four Noble Truths.

Mindfulness truly is the foundation of all of the teachings of the Buddha. By practicing mindfulness within the context of The Four Noble Truths, you can free yourself of the stress and suffering caused by mindlessness. Mindfulness within the context of The

155

Four Noble Truths will develop an awakened mind, a mind of pure equanimity.

The Buddha concluded his teaching on The Four Foundations of (Right) Mindfulness with a promise: "'This is the direct path for the purification of beings, for the overcoming of sorrow & lamentation, for the disappearance of pain & distress, for the attainment of the right method, & for the realization of Unbinding — in other words, the four frames of reference.' Thus was it said, and in reference to this was it said." [25]

Right Mindfulness is a refined mindfulness that supports refined thinking and deepening concentration.

The following section reviews Shamatha-Vipassana meditation within the context of the concentration factors of the Eightfold Path. This is to develop further the understanding of the importance of the entire framework of the Eightfold Path in successful development of an enlightened mind.

Right Meditation

You have been using Shamatha-Vipassana meditation throughout this course. As you have progressed you have begun to develop understanding of The Four Noble Truths and integrate the supportive framework of the Eightfold Path.

The Buddha taught that Right Meditation was Shamatha-Vipassana meditation practiced within the supportive framework of the Eightfold Path. The Eightfold Path provides the proper application of deepening concentration and refined mindfulness.

It is important here to remember that the purpose of The Eightfold Path is to understand unhappiness and stress and abandon clinging, craving, desire and aversion. To that end the Buddha taught a very simple and very profound and effective meditation practice.

Prior to settling on Shamatha-Vipassana meditation, the Buddha studied with the foremost meditation teachers of his time. He was taught and practiced the most advanced meditation techniques.

These techniques developed mind-states of nothingness and non-perception, still common meditation practices today. The Buddha found these techniques to lack the intention and framework necessary to develop understanding and cessation.

He found them lacking in developing a tranquil mind that would support gaining insight into impermanence, stress and the ego-self.

The Buddha found them all ineffective in developing Samadhi, a non-distracted quality of mind.

The Buddha found them lacking in developing knowledge of The Four Noble Truths.

Right Meditation will quickly develop two conditions that are essential to achieving the understanding of stress and the cessation of stress. These two conditions are Shamatha and Vipassana. Shamatha means serenity or tranquility, a quiet mind. A quiet and non-reactive mind is a mind resting in equanimity. Vipassana means insight. This is not an analytical type of insight but a dispassionate mindfulness of the true nature of stress, impermanence and the ego-personality within the framework of the Eightfold Path and in the context of The Four Noble Truths.

What you think, what is generated in your mind, is what you will experience. This is why quieting your mind and gaining insight into thoughts and thought constructs is so effective in developing understanding and wisdom.

Awareness into the confusing, impermanent, and delusional nature of your conditioned mind is the "insight" gained in vipassana. Always preceded by shamatha, a tranquil mind, you are able to be mindful of your conditioned thinking and put your conditioned thinking aside. Nothing else needs to be done or should be done with these fragments of conditioned thinking.

Conditioned thinking causes wrong perception or wrong view, which causes an unskillful reaction. This reaction creates further conditioned thinking. By using the insight gained by Shamatha-Vipassana you are able to recognize and let go of reaction and interrupt the cycle of discursive thinking.

No further analysis of your reactive thoughts or feelings is necessary, or even effective in breaking this pattern. Analysis of conditioned thinking during meditation can often strengthen reactive thinking.

Using any meditation practice to change the ego-self or seek pleasant mind states or mystical experiences will create more conditioned thinking. One can spend eternity in this pursuit, constantly creating the perception of change and understanding and never realizing a peaceful and non-distracted mind.

The purpose of shamatha-vipassana meditation is to put aside all conditioned mind states. Within the framework of The Eightfold Path, shamatha-vipassana meditation will develop Samadhi and profound and useful insight.

A mind easily distracted will be unable to recognize conditioned mind states. Conditioned mind arises and is reinforced by discriminating thoughts of craving and clinging to what brings pleasure, and aversion to disappointment, pain and suffering.

Shamatha-Vipassana meditation quickly develops the concentration necessary to recognize discursive and delusional thinking. Recognition of discursive and delusional thinking allows for the possibility of putting aside the cause of the stress and confusion that would otherwise continue to generate endless conditioned mind states.

Samadhi is a fundamental quality of mind that is essential to developing understanding of The Four Noble Truths. Developing understanding of The Four Noble Truths brings lasting peace and happiness. Samadhi means unwavering concentration. Samadhi is a non-distracted quality of mind that is developed through The Eightfold Path.

The Buddha identified the most basic human difficulty as dukkha. Dukkha is a pervasive and continually reoccurring phenomenon arising from ignorance and continued by craving and clinging.

Due to a belief and attachment to an ego-personality a distracted mind will constantly seek experiences that bring sense-pleasures and constantly avoid that which diminishes pleasure or brings disappointment and unhappiness. Not-Self or the ego-personality craves constant sensory stimulation. Often even momentary interruption to sensory stimulation brings an unsettled quality of mind known as boredom. Much of life is spent in activity simply to avoid boredom.

A significant difficulty in beginning a shamatha-vipassana meditation practice is boredom. Boredom is your ego-personality's need for constant sensory fulfillment not being fulfilled. When boredom arises in your mind simply acknowledge that boredom has arisen and return your mindfulness to your breath. This directly interrupts your conditioned mind's need for constant stimulation.

This need for constant stimulation is the distraction of dukkha. The Buddha understood that the continual reestablishment of the ego-personality in every thought maintains stress and unhappiness. The preoccupation with dukkha prevents lasting peace and happiness.

The Buddha considered carefully how he could teach this understanding. He taught The Four Noble Truths as a way to develop wisdom and understanding.

To reiterate, the purpose of shamatha-vipassana meditation within the framework of the Eightfold Path is to put aside the distraction of dukkha and develop Samadhi, a non-distracted quality of mind, and insight into impermanence, not-self, and stress.

The Buddha taught Samadhi in numerous Suttas, always describing the result of Samadhi. What is clear in all these teachings is the quality of mind the Buddha describes. These are qualities of an awakened mind fully present in the phenomenal world.

"Wise & mindful, you should develop immeasurable concentration. When, wise & mindful, one has developed immeasurable concentration, five realizations arise right within oneself. Which five?

"The realization arises within oneself that 'This concentration is blissful in the present and will result in bliss in the future.

"The realization arises within oneself that 'This concentration is noble & not connected with the baits of the flesh.'

"The realization arises within oneself that 'This concentration is not obtained by base people.

"The realization arises within oneself that 'This concentration is peaceful, exquisite, the acquiring of serenity, the attainment of unity, not kept in place by the fabrications of forceful restraint.

"The realization arises within oneself that 'I enter into this concentration mindfully, and mindfully I emerge from it.

"Wise & mindful, you should develop immeasurable concentration. When, wise & mindful, one has developed immeasurable concentration, these five realizations arise within oneself." [26]

Mindfulness as it relates to an awakened mind is described here. One enters into Samadhi with mindfulness AND emerges from Samadhi with mindfulness. This means that deep concentration is developed with Right Mindfulness and that Right Mindfulness remains during the day-to-day mundane activities of life.

This last answers the question of what becomes of the ego-personality upon awakening. The ego-personality, or Not-Self, is let go of, often called unbinding. A now fully-awakened human being remains mindful moment-by-moment, free of the distraction of dukkha.

In response to a question by Punnaka, a monk in the Sangha, regarding how to arrive "at the far shore" of awakening the Buddha again spoke of developing a non-distracted quality of mind:

"Friends, these are the four developments of concentration. Which four? There is the development of concentration that, when developed & pursued, leads to a pleasant abiding in the here & now.

"There is the development of concentration that, when developed & pursued, leads to the attainment of knowledge & vision.

"There is the development of concentration that, when developed & pursued, leads to mindfulness & alertness.

"There is the development of concentration that, when developed & pursued, leads to the ending of stress and unhappiness.

"And what is the development of concentration that, when developed & pursued, leads to a pleasant abiding in the here & now? One remains 'Equanimous & mindful, he has a pleasant abiding in the here & now." [27]

Here again the Buddha is describing the quality of an awakened mind, a mind settled in equanimity abiding with mindfulness of life as life occurs and within the context of The Four Noble Truths. By putting aside the cause of the distraction of dukkha one develops lasting peace and happiness.

"Friends, develop concentration. A concentrated mind discerns in line with what has come into being. And what does he discern in line with what has come into being? The origination & disappearance of feeling, the origination & disappearance of perception, origination &

disappearance of fabrications, the origination & disappearance of consciousness.

"In short the origination & disappearance of the five clinging-aggregates (the ego-personality)." [28]

The Five Clinging Aggregates are explained in week eight.

Insight is recognizing conditioned thinking and the impermanence of all things including thoughts. Being mindful of the breath brings tranquility which allows for recognition of distraction and discursive thinking. Refined mindfulness is the ability to dispassionately maintain Right View and to remain in a non-distracted mind state.

Your ego-self, what the Buddha teaches is anatta, not a self, constantly seeks to establish itself in every object, event, view, or idea that occurs. As all objects, events, views, and ideas are impermanent and unsatisfactory, constant distraction becomes the remedy for the underlying unsatisfactory nature of life. This is dukkha.

A well-concentrated mind resting in dispassionate mindfulness seeks nothing and remains free of distraction driven by the needs of an ego-personality. This is the end of craving and clinging. This is an awakened mind.

Establishing and maintaining shamatha-vipassana meditation within the framework of The Eightfold Path will develop lasting happiness and peace.

Shamatha-Vipassana meditation is a simple method with profound and transformative results. It is a method that anyone can integrate into their lives. Within the framework of The Eightfold Path, shamatha-vipassana meditation will develop the insight necessary to put aside all delusional and discursive thinking.

The Eightfold Path is the framework for putting aside the distractions caused by desire. It is the distraction and confusion arising from clinging that perpetuates dukkha and blocks awakening.

This simple though profound practice of developing heightened wisdom, heightened virtue and heightened concentration is the most precious teaching of the world's most insightful thinker.

"And this, monks, is the noble truth of the way of practice leading to the cessation of dukkha: precisely this Noble Eightfold Path: right view, right intention, right speech, right action, right livelihood, right effort, right mindfulness, right meditation."[29]

Remember, with Shamatha-Vipassana meditation you are not seeking a trance-like state or an avoidance of thinking. You are not attempting to develop a mind-state of "nothingness." While it is possible to set an intention to use meditation to manipulate a mind-state of nothingness, nothingness is a mind-state similar to unconsciousness. This mind-state may even seem pleasant as it is an escape from what is occurring.

There is no useful development of insight into The Four Noble Truths or Impermanence, Not-Self, and Stress from a mind-state of nothingness, or similar mind-states. Useful and effective insight is developed with Shamatha-Vipassana meditation within the framework of the Eightfold Path.

The purpose of Shamatha-Vipassana meditation is primarily to develop concentration. Every time you find yourself caught up in your thinking and then return your mindfulness to your breath you are interrupting conditioned thinking and deepening concentration.

The wisdom of The Eightfold Path, beginning with Right View and Right Intention, supported by virtuous behavior, develops heightened Samadhi. A non-distracted mind is a mind at peace. A mind at peace, free of the constant need to maintain an ego-personality abides in lasting happiness.

Right Meditation is informed and supported by the other seven factors of The Eightfold Path. Samadhi is the quality of mindfulness that rests in the understanding of The Four Noble Truths.

Developing samadhi, non-distraction, using Shamatha-Vipassana meditation within the framework of the Eightfold Path is the task associated with Right Meditation.

This Week's Dhamma Study

- Listen to the week six talk on Right Effort, Right Mindfulness and Right Meditation:
  http://crossrivermeditation.com/truth-of-happiness-online-course-talks/

- Continue with your meditation practice in the morning and early evening. If you feel comfortable with adding a few minutes to your practice do so. Five to ten minutes of meditation each session should be comfortable now.

- In meditation, remain mindful of your breathing as you dispassionately notice feelings and thoughts arise and dissipate. When you notice that you are caught up in your own thoughts and have lost awareness of your breath, put aside the focus on your thoughts and place your awareness on your breathing. Continue to be aware of your mind from a dispassionate observational view, a mind-state of choiceless awareness always mindful of your breath.

- At the end of your meditation sessions take a moment to notice the quality of your mind. Be at peace with the quality of your mind.

- Continue to develop wisdom by noticing your attachments to the people and events of your life, including yourself. Continue to generate the Right Intention to let go of all attachments and all impermanent views.

- In your day-to-day life notice when you are engaged in Right Speech, Right Action and Right Livelihood and when you are not. Develop the strong intention to abandon all wrong speech, action and livelihood. As concentration deepens, non-virtuous thoughts, words and deeds become apparent.

- Continue to develop Right Effort. Put aside time for a consistent meditation practice and maintain a priority to your practice. There will always be life events distracting away from practice. Very rarely will these events be more immediate or important than putting aside time twice a day for a period of meditation. Bring mindfulness into all areas of your life by staying focused in the present moment.

- Notice any persistent thoughts and your awareness of the impermanence of all thoughts. Avoid being analytical. This is a dispassionate observance of thoughts and feelings as they arise and pass away. Take note of developing a more mindful presence in your life. Notice when you are fully present with another. Notice when you are not as distracted or reactive.

- Continue your Dhamma study with week seven.

- Always be gentle with yourself and enjoy your practice!

If taking the correspondence course:

- Write a paragraph or two regarding your Dhamma practice and write down any questions or insights into incorporating Right Effort, Right Mindfulness and Right Meditation into your life.

- To submit your writing, please use this form: http://crossrivermeditation.com/home-study-submissions/

- I will respond to you within 24 to 48 hours.

Week Seven
Anicca, Anatta, and Dukkha

Impermanence,

The Not-Self Characteristic,

and Stress

You now have established a useful and effective meditation practice within the context of The Four Noble Truths and the refined framework of the Eightfold Path. In order to develop lasting peace and happiness, complete understanding of the nature of unsatisfactory and confusing experiences will now be developed.

In order to develop understanding of dukkha, understanding the impermanent environment of all human experience, and the "self" experiencing dukkha within this environment, will also be developed. In essence, each of these three discrete characteristic includes the other two characteristics.

This week's study of Impermanence, Not-Self, and Stress, and next week's study of Dependent Origination and The Five Clinging-Aggregates will develop understanding of these teachings within the proper context, and with heightened concentration and refined mindfulness.

I will first describe anicca, anatta, and dukkha separately and then describe the ongoing interplay of these three "Marks of Existence." The first two characteristics, anicca and anatta, are animate while dukkha is inanimate as a description of the result of the first two. It will be seen, though, that dukkha has an animating characteristic due to the reaction to stress within the conditioned mind of anatta.

During this week's study, and next week's too, I will place some emphasis on the contradictions between the Buddha's direct teachings and modern Buddhist doctrine. I include this only for clarity and context. I intend no disrespect for the later-developed teachings, or of any individual teacher.

Anicca

The Impermanence Characteristic

"Be mindful of impermanence to end conceit. When impermanence is understood it is also understood that none of this is self. Understanding not-self uproots conceit, uproots I-making. When fully established release is complete." [30]

Impermanence is an essential concept of the Dhamma. Impermanence describes the environment in which unhappiness and stress arises and is maintained. All things in the phenomenal world are impermanent and all events are uncertain as to occurrence, effect and duration. Even your view of yourself changes from moment to moment.

Understanding that all things are impermanent, including self-referential thoughts, is the key to understanding how your thinking has created the condition of stress.

Some physical objects, such as a mountain, or planet, or the universe, maintain a physical form for a longer period of time than a butterfly, an apple, a thought, or a human body. All will decay, change form, and fade from existence.

Another way of describing the impermanence of all phenomenal things is that uncertainty is characteristic of all phenomenal things. We can never know what the next moment will bring. Ignorance of uncertainty develops additional clinging and additional stress. Wisdom is knowing, understanding, and accepting impermanence and uncertainty. Wisdom brings a mind of calm and spacious equanimity.

The importance of understanding impermanence cannot be overstated. It was impermanence that the Buddha spoke of in his last teaching: "Impermanent are all conditioned things. Decay is relentless. Work diligently for your own understanding." [31]

The Buddha understood the impermanence of all things in the phenomenal world but did not over-emphasize phenomenal impermanence or creating anything special regarding the general impermanence of the world. He placed emphasis on understanding the impermanence of what is commonly viewed as a self and the self's relationship with the impermanence of the phenomenal world.

"Friends, form (physical objects and the physical body) is like foam. Seeing clearly, form is empty and without substance. Whether past, present or future, internal, external, subtle or obvious, seeing form as it is, like foam on the water, brings wisdom to the well-instructed. Clearly seeing they become disenchanted with form, disenchanted with feeling, disenchanted with perception, disenchanted with fabrications and disenchanted with consciousness. Disenchanted one grows dispassionate. With dispassion comes release (from craving and clinging.)

Form, feelings, perceptions, fabrications, and consciousness are the five factors of the Five Clinging-Aggregates that is explained in context of Dependent Origination in week eight. It is mentioned here to also develop the understanding of the relationship between "not-self," impermanence, and stress.

"Friends, when a learned follower has heard the truth and understands the truth they will no longer cling to form, or to feeling, or to perceptions, or to fabrications, or to the flow of thoughts. They will see clearly 'this is not me, this is not mine, this is not myself.' They are fully released." [32]

The strong self-referential view of self as a substantial and sustainable physical entity animated by a likewise self-referential consciousness is initially difficult to understand abandon. By developing concentration and refined mindfulness through the Eightfold Path this ongoing process can be clearly observed and abandoned.

As all things are impermanent and without any sustainable substance, like foam on the water, it is foolish to cling to anything, including form, feelings, perceptions, fabrications, or any thought.

Anatta

The Not-Self Characteristic

Anatta is the word the Buddha used to describe what is commonly referred to as "self." The Buddha describes the mental-physical ego-self as "anatta" to show the impermanent, ever-changing, insubstantiality of the conditioned ego-personality. What is thought of as self, as me or mine, is a deluded view rooted in ignorance (of the Four Noble Truths.)

Anatta, the not-self characteristic, is unique to the teachings of the Buddha, and perhaps the most difficult to observe and understand. The more conditioned thinking is established, the more difficult it will be to grasp this third observable truth.

If you look closely at what you normally view as "self" you will see that there is nothing permanent that you can perceive through your five physical senses and interpretive consciousness, or the six-sense base. (*The six-sense base is your five physical senses interpreted and moderated by your thoughts.*)

This is a kind of feedback loop, or discursive thinking: From wrong view (or ignorant view, lacking wisdom) you perceive yourself through contact with your senses as the "perceiver" and all perceived phenomenon as outside of yourself, therefore you must in fact have a permanent and separate existence from other observed phenomenon that appear "outside" of you the "perceiver."

This wrong view can only perpetuate wrong view. Ignorance can never lead to wisdom, only wisdom ends ignorance. Though firmly entrenched in the human psyche the belief in an ego-self as a permanent and sustainable individual entity is a wrong view and leads to endless confusion and suffering.

What is perceived as a self is an ego-personality that has arisen from certain conditions known as the "12 Links of Dependent Origination." The ego-personality is the mental-physical form arisen from wrong view and maintained by clinging to wrong views.

Dependent Origination is explained in detail in week eight. I will also refer to not-self (non-self) as ego-self or ego-personality. Anatta is first presented here in context of Anicca and Dukkha, and is explained in week eight in the context of Dependent Origination.

Any further establishment of self-identity in any form or in any realm, physical or non-physical, will only lead to more confusion and suffering. This includes modern Buddhist doctrines of an inherent Buddha-nature or the self achieving Buddhahood. These notions are merely creating another conceptual (imaginary) framework to house the ego-personality and are contrary to the Buddha's Dhamma.

Not-Self has also been misinterpreted and misapplied in some modern Buddhist schools to mean that the self is nothing, or a void, and has led some schools to create a doctrine of "nothingness" or "emptiness." Not-Self simply means that what is commonly viewed as "self" is impermanent and insubstantial and requires a continual process of "I-making," or conceit to continue. This is a wrong view arising from ignorance. What is commonly viewed as a self is Anatta, Not-a-Self.

The Buddha did not teach that there is no self, only that the self fabricated through an observable process is not worth defending or continually re-establishing. Anatta, not-self, refers, to your ego-personality. It is your ego-personality that is prone to endless confusion and suffering. Though insubstantial and ever-changing, your ego-self's sole purpose is to continue to establish its "self" in every object, event, view, or idea. Anatta has created endless views of itself that are all subject to impermanence and suffering. It is in this underlying impermanence that the pervasive unsatisfactory experience of dukkha arises and is maintained.

Insight into this one thing, that all views arising from an ego-self cause stress and unhappiness, brings understanding and lasting peace and happiness. Within the framework of The Eightfold Path all views of self are recognized. As new views arise they are quickly abandoned. It is not-self, your ego-personality, that is subject to stress. It is only this impermanent and insubstantial ego-personality that is to be abandoned. This is why all views of self are to be recognized and abandoned. This is the purpose of insight: to clearly recognize impermanence and all wrong views of self.

The simplest way to describe the Buddha's teaching on Not-self is this: anything that the ego-self clings to, whether objects, people, events, views, or ideas, or craving through the pursuit of happiness through acquisition of objects, people, events, views, or ideas, will create confusion, disenchantment and lasting unhappiness - let all craving and clinging views go.

Still another way to see this is by definition and association. The self is defined by attachments. Association is another word for attachments. Who you associate with and what you associate with defines the self you will experience. This does not mean that you should have no associations. It does mean you should be mindful of all associations and to not try to make what is impermanent permanent. As clinging to an ego-personality ceases, self-identification through associations also ceases.

Do your associations support developing understanding within the framework of The Eightfold Path? Do your associations increase your own and other's confusion and suffering through validation of yours and other's unskillful actions? The Eightfold Path provides a highly effective framework for guiding associations and focus for practice.

Once clinging is recognized and abandoned, you will no longer cling to others. This brings the ability to be mindfully present in the world and with others with no expectations or insistence that your life, or the people in your life, including yourself, be any different than what is occurring.

All aspects of self are impermanent and any conditioned thought or thought construct that attempts to distract from this truth is also clinging, specifically clinging to views and ideas. Clinging to views and ideas maintains the distraction of stress and generates kamma.

Kamma and rebirth are explained in week nine.

Anatta, not-self, continually seeks to establish itself in impermanent objects, views, and ideas. This is the purpose of the phenomenal world and why the ego-self is so enamored with the world. As long as anatta continues this quest, confusion and suffering will prevail. As long as anatta continues this quest, kamma will continue.

183

Due to unquenched desire for existence, the ego-personality creates kamma. Kamma (Sanskrit: Karma) unfolds moment-by-moment as the distraction of stress and unhappiness. Though physical form will change due to impermanence, kamma continues the experience of stress and unhappiness.

This is an important example of impermanence as impermanence relates to anatta. Continuity is not permanence. Continuity is recurrence due to repeatedly recreating the conditions leading to an experience, in this case continued re-establishment of an ego-self subject to confusion and suffering.

Recurring life situations and intellectual or emotional reactions are simply an impermanent, but repetitive, and discursive, product of discriminating consciousness, or conditioned mind. Conditioned thinking and conditioned mind is formed due to ignorance of impermanence, maintained by the distraction of stress, and given validity by an ego-personality.

Continuity caused by clinging conditioned mind is ongoing Dukkha.

Dukkha

The Unsatisfactory Characteristic

Dukkha is a Pali word that means unsatisfactory, uncertain, disappointing, stress, confusion, and all manner of mental and physical suffering rooted in self-referential views. I will use these words interchangeably to signify dukkha.

"Birth is dukkha, aging is dukkha, death is dukkha; sorrow, lamentation, pain, grief, & despair are dukkha; association with the un-beloved is dukkha; separation from the loved is dukkha; not getting what is wanted is dukkha. In short, the Five Clinging-Aggregates are dukkha." [33]

The common human problem is the underlying general unsatisfactory nature of human life. This is Dukkha. Included in Dukkha is all manner of unsatisfactoriness, from mild disappointment to the most extreme physical and emotional distress. While extreme experiences of dukkha are somewhat individual, dukkha is a common human experience that no one can avoid.

All human beings are subject to sickness, aging and death, Along the way all are subject to unsatisfactory, disappointing and unpleasant experiences. Even pleasant experiences have an underlying unsatisfactory aspect due to impermanence and uncertainty. The ego-personality develops clinging to pleasure-giving experiences, creating stress. A form of clinging is aversion to unpleasant experiences, also contributing stress.

Dukkha is both an experience of interaction with the impermanent environment that the self is a part of, and the self. This is an important point to be developed. Once the understanding that it is the (wrong) view of self that is the cause of confusion, stress and ongoing delusion, these views can now be mindfully abandoned.

"There are these three forms of stress, my friend: the stress of pain, the stress of fabrication, the stress of change. These are the three forms of stress." 34

It is the ego-personality, what is shown to be anatta, not-a-self, that experiences the three forms of stress. To re-state the Four Noble Truths in this context, there is an underlying and pervasive unsatisfactoriness to life that the ego-self experiences.

As the experiencer (you) is also linked to the experience and the environment that the experience arises, the self is impermanent and the wrong view of self is also dukkha.

It is due to the effects of stress that make understanding stress paramount in the Buddha's teaching. It is preoccupation with stress that prevents awakening. It is the preoccupation with the need to continually establish and defend your impermanent, ever-changing, ego-personality that continues confusion and stress.

Jambukhadika the wanderer asks the Buddha: "What is the path, what is the practice for the full comprehension of these forms of stressfulness?"

"Precisely this Noble Eightfold Path, my friend — right view, right resolve, right speech, right action, right livelihood, right effort, right mindfulness, right meditation. This is the path, this is the practice for the full comprehension of these forms of stressfulness." [35]

In describing the refined mindfulness of an awakened mind the Buddha stated "Dukkha is understood." [4] Understanding dukkha and how impermanence and your ego-personality become intertwined in proliferating dukkha is developed through the Eightfold Path.

Understanding The Interdependence Of Anicca, Anatta, and Dukkha

Interdependence, inter-connectedness, and inter-being are words commonly used in modern Buddhism. Using these words to create a doctrine of universal sameness or the inter-connectedness of all phenomenon, including creating a doctrine of the interconnectedness, or inter-being, of impermanent and insubstantial ego-personality's, is contrary to the Buddha's teaching and develops additional clinging. These modern Buddhist doctrines arise from a misunderstanding and misapplication of Dependent Origination. These doctrines seek to establish Anatta, Not-A-Self, in a manner that only creates additional confusion and suffering.

It is deluded thinking to create a cosmic doctrine of interdependence, inter-connectedness, or inter-being.

Anicca, Anatta, and Dukkha are the three linked characteristics of human life. In this context they are inter-connected and interdependent. This is only to state the truth of life in the phenomenal world so that understanding of Dukkha and the effects of craving and clinging can be developed. Once this understanding is developed, the confusion and stress inherent in these three linked characteristics can be mindfully ended.

Interdependence in the context of The Four Noble Truths applies only to the relationship of these three "Marks of Existence."

Anicca, impermanence; Anatta, not-self; and Dukkha, stress, unsatisfactoriness; are the three linked characteristics of life in the phenomenal world. Impermanence, not-self, and stress are also known as "The Three Marks of Existence." All of life is impermanent and impersonal, lacking a definable self. It is through the establishment of an impermanent ego-self within an impermanent environment that initiates the underlying and pervasive unsatisfactory experience of human life.

Understanding these three characteristics, and their interdependence, is developed within the framework of The Eightfold Path. The Eightfold Path directly develops the understanding of "I-making" within an impermanent environment, and the subsequent unsatisfactory experience of the ego-self.

The sole purpose of the Dhamma is to recognize and abandon craving and all clinging views of an ego-self. Craving and clinging causes the confusion and distraction of Dukkha. Abandoning craving and clinging brings an end to Dukkha.

"Free of craving and clinging one is not agitated. Un-agitated this one is totally unbound and free of Dukkha, an Arahant." [36]

As concentration increases through shamatha-vipassana meditation the process of establishing and maintaining an ego-self is able to be mindfully observed. Once this process is recognized, with Right Intention, and the other mutually-supportive factors of the Eightfold Path, the continual establishment and defense of your ego-self is finally abandoned.

Impermanence, stress, and the ego-self are all observable facts of human existence. What the Buddha discovered upon his awakening, with a quiet and well-concentrated mind, is that all things are conditioned particles of energy that have coalesced into the appearance of form. Out of the formless state we now have form. The seemingly separate forms that we perceive are impermanent and absent of any self-inherent nature, including the form we perceive as "I."

It requires continued, ever-vigilant directed thought to maintain the ego-self in an impermanent environment. Another way of saying this is clinging to form. This is stress. This is dukkha.

This confused and conditioned thinking can be refined and purified and bring relief from craving and clinging.

Prior to his awakening, the future Buddha wandered northern India with five colleagues, all seeking understanding. Kondanna was one of the Buddha's five colleagues. A few weeks after his awakening the Buddha presented The Four Noble Truths to Kondanna and the other four seekers. Upon hearing this first discourse of the Buddha, Kondanna declared "All conditioned things (including self) that arise are subject to cessation." The Buddha recognized Kondanna's accomplishment saying: "So you really know, Kondanna, you really know. You are now Anna-Kondanna, Kondanna who knows." [37]

The cause of the unsatisfactory nature of life is rooted in the deluded belief in a fixed and permanent mental-physical self, the self-referential ego-self. Craving for the establishment of a self and clinging to the perception of an established self initiates the unsatisfactory nature of life.

What has arisen within an impermanent environment cannot be seen to have any permanent or substantial characteristic. The discrete components that join, or cling together, to have the appearance of permanent individuality is like an illusion. It is only in the clinging-together of discrete components, or aggregates, that a self seems to be established. None of the aggregates are permanent or substantial and there is no permanence or substantiality achieved in the coming-together of the components.

Much like a chair deconstructed to its component parts would no longer have characteristics of a chair, a human form deconstructed to its component parts could no longer be identified as a individual "self." The chairs identity is linked to all of its component parts coming together in a certain form.

A pile of a chair's components could not be called a chair. It is only in the impermanent coming-together that the discrete components are identified as a chair.

When a chair is de-constructed, whether intentionally or with the progression of time, it no longer has the characteristics of a chair. In other words, the characterization of the present state of the chair as a chair can only truthfully refer to what is being observed through a current view is a chair. Nothing can be seen in the form of a chair that provides the chair with any lasting validity except for the common agreement of its use.

Identification as a self is dependent on this phenomenon as well. The human body holding a "consciousness" that is perceived to be a "self" is just as "empty" of a permanent identify as its deconstructed components. Since none of the individual components can be said to have a "self," it is only in the clinging together of the discrete components, or individual aggregates, that we say that the body houses a separate and unique self.

The human form is a discrete component of the physical universe that has arisen to interact with the physical world and is dependent on the same causes and conditions of all phenomena for its existence. This mental-physical ego-self, subject to the same truth as all physical phenomena, arises from the formless, becomes form, and will again enter the formless state.

The wisdom of the Dhamma shows the foolishness to cling an identity to a form that is impermanent and insubstantial, and prone to confusion and stress.

This mental-physical form, rooted in ignorance, acquires the characteristics that craving directs it towards through seeking sensory satisfaction. Clinging establishes and maintains this form by holding on to sensory fulfillment.

This course and the Buddha's dhamma brings insight into this process. Complete development of the Eightfold Path brings release from the process of continual "I-making."

Through understanding the environment in which the ego-personality is established and maintained, all views of self can be recognized. Through recognition and Right Intention all views of self can be abandoned. The Eightfold Path develops understanding and profound Right View. Right View is understanding the truth of stress and the impermanent environment in which the ego-self is established and maintained.

The ego-personality is associated with a physical form that is interpreted through consciousness. This combination of consciousness and form is known as Nama-Rupa. Nama-Rupa means Name and Form. Name, or Nama, (conscious identity or identification as an ego-personality) is the mental or psychological factor of an ego-self and Rupa, form, is the physical factor. This mental/physical self is an aggregate of five impermanent phenomenal aspects that together comprise what is called a self. There is nothing permanent about any individual aspect of the five aggregates nor in the combination of all five.

These five factors of not-self, known as "The Five Clinging Aggregates" are:

1. Physical Form
2. Feelings
3. Perceptions
4. Mental Fabrications
5. Consciousness

The Five Clinging-Aggregates is explained in detail in week Eight. I am introducing this here to establish the context within a general explanation of anicca, anatta, and dukkha.

The Buddha's teaching on what constitutes a self has taken on confusing and misleading esoteric, magical and mystical interpretations. Anatta means "not-self" or "non-self" and refers to that which is to be abandoned through understanding and developing The Four Noble Truths. It would be (and is) confusing to attempt to describe a concept of self without the context of developing an understanding of The Four Noble Truths.

It is in the continual attempt to establish and maintain an ego-self within the environment of impermanence that perpetuates dukkha. Some "Buddhist" practices do just this by over-emphasis on conceptual notions of not-self, "nothingness" and "emptiness" and creating mystical connotations to non-self. One example of this is the notion of an inner or obscured Buddha-nature that spontaneously arises following sufficient effort. Another example is a "Buddha-Hood" that the ego-personality should aspire to. Both of these confused doctrines assume an obscure but permanent and substantial "self" within what the Buddha taught was "Anatta."

There is nothing that can be shown to have any permanence, including a "Buddha-nature" or "Buddha-hood," residing within an impermanent ego-personality. There is no teaching of the Buddha's that seeks to uncover a hidden Buddha-nature or latent Buddha-hood.

Still one more example is the notion of a PureLand Buddhist heaven that if the proper conditions are met by the ego-personality during physical life, a special type of Buddha called Amitabha-Buddha, lord of the PureLand, will welcome and provide an environment of everlasting bliss to house the (impermanent) ego-personality.

These notions serve only to establish the ego-self in a conceptual realm that is also subject to further confusion and suffering.

The refined mindfulness developed through the Eightfold Path brings an understanding of all impermanent views and ideas rooted in ignorance. Awakening brings the end of deluded views.

In modern Buddhism misunderstanding the process for how all things in the phenomenal world are inter-connected has led to a subtle but distraction-causing over-emphasis on interconnectedness. Due to the nature of how an ego-self arises and perceives, all objects are inter-connected, but all objects are also impermanent and insubstantial. Creating a conceptual and false doctrine of interconnectedness, interdependence, or inter-being only fosters clinging and promotes additional confusion, delusion, and suffering.

The Buddha consistently avoided the myriad attempts at establishing anatta in endless conceptual realms as this would prove a distraction to his stated purpose. "Not-self" simply refers to an insubstantial and impermanent ego-personality that is mistaken as a substantial and permanent individual identity.

Rather than creating a distracting and misinformed doctrine of nothingness or emptiness, the Eightfold Path brings understanding of the process of giving birth to an impermanent ego-self rooted in ignorance and prone to endless confusion and suffering, and presents the clear and practical path of developing profound wisdom of the continuity of unconditioned mindful experience.

The suffering caused by ignorance should not be further ignored but it should be seen that creating specialness of impermanent objects, events, views, and ideas due to phenomenal inter-connection perpetuates distraction and stress. Ignoring Right View that would bring insight into ignorance is delusion. Anatta, your ego-personality, insists on ignoring any teaching that would diminish its hold on delusion.

Any further establishment of anatta, the ego-self, in any realm to support any idea or ideal will only create further confusion and suffering as it encourages further craving and clinging. This includes the establishment of a "special" or "advanced" type of Buddhist Practice. The Buddha taught a common solution to the common human problem of Dukkha. He taught that Anatta, the ego-self, is maintained by craving and clinging. This includes self-referential views that cling" the self to forms, feelings, thoughts, and later-developed doctrines.

Through the development of all factors of The Eightfold Path, insight into impermanence, uncertainty and clinging arises. Understanding how ignorance contributes to the establishment and maintenance of a "self" develops the ability to abandon all views of self.

These are not abstract, mystical, magical, or esoteric ideas. Holding Right View and Right Intention brings virtuous thoughts, words, and deeds. Remaining mindful of Right Speech, Right Action and Right Livelihood, insight into craving and clinging is developed. Developing Right Concentration by engaging in Right Effort, Right Mindfulness and Right Meditation will develop insight into impermanence, unsatisfactoriness, and your ego-self.

199

It is possible to understand abandon the process of the establishment of "not-self." Releasing the clinging necessary to maintain the deluded views of self is awakening. The Buddha describes awakening simply and directly, without any ambiguity, esoterica, or magical thinking:

"Awakening is understanding stress, abandoning the cause of stress (craving and clinging), experiencing the cessation of stress, and developing the path leading to the cessation of stress." [38]

As has been seen, the ego-self is also included as dukkha. Developing profound understanding of what appears as a "self," and ending craving and clinging, is awakening.

Understanding impermanence brings an end to all clinging views. Impermanence is the pervasive, over-arching experience of all life in the phenomenal world. By clinging to the form of an ego-self, stress is experienced within the environment of impermanence through perception and feeling, and reactive and distracted thinking. The ego-personality establishes and maintains itself by clinging to impermanent objects, events, views, and ideas. It is your ego-personality that is subject to unhappiness and stress.

As the way of understanding the environment of impermanence and clinging the Buddha taught Four Noble Truths. The development and understanding of The Four Noble Truths occurs within the environment of impermanence. The significance of this is that the Eightfold Path is not a way to manage or avoid stress and confusion but to develop profound understanding of the process that develops confusion and stress so that confusion and stress can be abandoned.

Having arisen within impermanence, the ego-self has the characteristics of impermanence. Not-Self is what is subject to the distraction of dukkha, perpetuating delusion. It is the establishment and maintenance of the ego-self that continues stress. It is within the environment of impermanence that stress arises and all wrong views of self are established and maintained. It is also within the environment of impermanence that awakening occurs.

Impermanence also allows for the ego-self to be extinguished and the distraction of stress brought to an end. Views of self leading to suffering are formed due to a lack of understanding, due to ignorance. Developing understanding, developing wisdom, ends unhappiness and stress.

It is clinging that perpetuates the ego-self. It is the ego-personality's preoccupation with stress that perpetuates clinging and continues disenchantment and unhappiness. This is self-perpetuating discursive thinking that conditioned mind continues through reaction and distraction.

Not-self refers to the impermanence and insubstantiality of the ego-personality. The insubstantiality of the ego-self is obscured by the preoccupation of maintaining anatta within the impermanent environment of stress. The stress and unsatisfactory nature of the ego-self is an underlying characteristic of the experience of life in the phenomenal world. In short anatta rooted in ignorance and impermanence is dukkha.

Shedding the ego-personality by ceasing clinging to impermanent objects and ignorant views brings lasting peace and happiness.

Understanding impermanence, stress and your ego-self is fundamental to understanding the Dhamma and developing The Noble Eightfold Path. Awakening is understanding the nature of experience in the phenomenal world and developing a profound understanding of The Four Noble Truths. The phenomenal world is all that is perceived through contact with the five physical senses and discriminating consciousness.

Worldly phenomena require certain conditions as pre-requisite for existence. When these conditions are no longer in effect, the manifestation of the conditions cease. As will be seen in the next chapter, the pre-requisite for anatta, for your ego-personality, is ignorance of the Four Noble Truths.

As wisdom of impermanence arises the conditions for the establishment of anatta are mindfully abandoned. Grasping and attachment ceases. Your ego-self, once dependent on ignorance giving rise to craving and clinging, no longer has the conditions present that are necessary for continuance. Confusion and suffering ends.

Look closely at anything with a form, and you will find that it is also formless, without any permanent characteristics. What has a form will also be formless. Out of formlessness, form appears. (This teaches impermanence, not emptiness.)

Initially it is desire for existence that conditioned mind arises. Continued grasping after contentment and pleasure, and maintaining aversion to what is uncomfortable or unpleasant reinforces conditioned mind. The Eightfold Path interrupts the self-perpetuating nature of conditioned mind.

If it were not for the truth of impermanence you could not liberate yourself from stress. You would be bound endlessly to disappointment, stress, dissatisfaction and suffering caused by your initial craving and clinging to phenomenon.

It is an obvious fact that all things are impermanent but the ego-personality continues to hold on to that which brings safety, pleasure and fulfillment, and develops aversion (clinging to avoidance) towards people and events it wishes to avoid.

It is this constant preoccupation with craving and clinging that maintains a self subject to suffering.

By using shamatha-vipassana meditation within the framework of The Eightfold Path insight is gained to the impermanent nature of thoughts and of all phenomena. Wisdom arises and all delusional thoughts are observed directly. The nature of impermanence, stress and the ego-self is understood with true and refined mindfulness.

Through the heightened wisdom gained from a Dhamma practice of heightened virtue and heightened concentration, the impermanence of all things is realized. Once impermanence is completely understood, the ego-self falls away as insubstantial and unsustainable. As the ego-self is abandoned through wisdom, craving and clinging ceases and stress and unhappiness comes to an end.

With no impermanent ego-self clinging to objects, views, and ideas, lasting peace and happiness arises within your once confused conditioned mind.

"The perceiving of impermanence, bikkhus, developed and frequently practiced, removes all sensual passion, removes all passion for material existence, removes all passion for becoming, removes all ignorance, removes and abolishes all conceit of "I am."

"Just as in the autumn a farmer, plowing with a large plow, cuts through all the spreading rootlets as he plows; in the same way, my dear friends, the perceiving of impermanence, developed and frequently practiced, removes all sensual passion... removes and abolishes all conceit of "I am." The Buddha [39]

This Week's Dhamma Study

- Listen to the week seven talk on Impermanence, Stress and Not-Self:
  http://crossrivermeditation.com/truth-of-happiness-online-course-talks/

- Continue with your meditation practice in the morning and early evening. If you feel comfortable with adding a few minutes to your practice do so. 10 to 15 minutes of meditation each session should be comfortable now.

- In meditation, remain mindful of your breathing as you dispassionately notice feelings and thoughts arise and dissipate. When you notice that you are caught up in your own thoughts and have lost awareness of your breath, put aside the focus on your thoughts and place your awareness on your breathing.

- At the end of your meditation sessions take a moment to notice the quality of your mind. Be at peace with the quality of your mind.

- Continue to be aware of your mind from a dispassionate observational view, a mind-state of choiceless awareness always mindful of your breath.

- Continue to develop wisdom by noticing your attachments to the people and events of your life, including yourself. Continue to generate the Right Intention to let go of all attachments and all impermanent views.

- In your day-to-day life notice when you are engaged in Right Speech, Right Action and Right Livelihood and when you are not. Develop the strong intention to abandon all wrong speech, wrong action, and wrong livelihood. As concentration deepens, non-virtuous thoughts, words and deeds become apparent.

- Continue to develop Right Effort. Put aside time for a consistent meditation practice and maintain a priority to your practice. There will always be life events distracting away from practice. Very rarely will these events be more immediate or important than putting aside time twice a day for a period of meditation. Bring mindfulness into all areas of your life by remaining mindful of what is occurring.

- Notice any persistent thoughts and your awareness of the impermanence of all thoughts. Avoid being analytical. This is a dispassionate observance of thoughts and feelings as they arise and pass away. Take note of developing a more mindful presence in your life. Notice when you are fully present with another. Notice when you are not as distracted or reactive.

- Continue your Dhamma study with week eight.

- Always be gentle with yourself and enjoy your practice!

If taking the correspondence course:

- Write a paragraph or two regarding your Dhamma practice and write down any questions or insights into impermanence and how impermanence contributes to stress and unhappiness. Note your deepening understanding of how impermanence and clinging give rise to the stress and unhappiness of the ego-personality.

- To submit your writing, please use this form: http://crossrivermeditation.com/home-study-submissions/

- I will respond to you within 24 to 48 hours.

Week Eight
Dependent Origination
and
The Five Clinging-Aggregates

The Truth of Not-Self

"As worldly phenomena is understood, the wise disciple, ever ardent and aware, resting in non-distraction, all their doubts vanish, when the cause of phenomena is rightly discerned." [40]

This week the teachings on Dependent Origination and The Five Clinging-Aggregates is presented. These are key understandings to develop and there is much information to absorb. You may want to take more than one week to study and begin to integrate these teachings. Please feel free to do so.

The Five Clinging-Aggregates are the Buddha's teachings on what constitutes the mental/physical form that appears to be the self. The Five Clinging-Aggregates are the impermanent components that, through clinging, cause the appearance of an individual form.

Dependent Origination (Dependent Co-arising) teaches understanding of the ongoing process of 12 causative links that establish and maintain delusion, confusion, and the underlying unsatisfactory experience of life.

The origination of delusion, confusion, and unsatisfactoriness that is experienced by a "self" is rooted in ignorance of the Four Noble Truths. Each individual link in the 12-link chain of dependencies is an observable component of the Five Clinging-Aggregates. The Five-Clinging-Aggregates are "dependent" on ignorance for the establishment of confusion and stress that results in the experience of craving and clinging. Developing understanding of The Four Noble Truths develops the wisdom that ends ignorance.

The importance of these teachings is to understand that the origination of all clinging views of an ego-self are rooted in ignorance. Once understood, craving and clinging can be abandoned and the 12 causative links in the chain of dependencies unbound. The process of ongoing confusion and stress comes to an end.

As all dukkha originates from the 12 links of Dependent Origination, we will start there.

The Buddha awakened to the profound understanding that from ignorance, through twelve observable causative conditions the ongoing process of stress and suffering is formed. He summarized this understanding when he presented his first teaching.

The Buddha's first discourse was the foundational teachings of The Four Noble Truths. The Four Noble Truths summarize the entire Dhamma. The first noble truth describes the condition caused by ignorance, the noble truth of dukkha (unsatisfactoriness, stress, unhappiness, disenchantment). The second noble truth describes the truth of craving and clinging as the origination of dukkha. The third noble truth states that cessation of dukkha is possible. The fourth noble truth is the truth of the Eightfold Path leading to the cessation of dukkha.

It is the development of The Eightfold Path that unbinds attachment, ends dukkha and brings awakening.

Nibbana (Sanskrit: Nirvana) is a Pali word, that describes the awakened mind state. Nibbana means extinguished or unbinding. Cessation of dukkha is the extinguishing of all wrong views that initiate craving and the unbinding of all clinging attachments.

As explained in the previous chapter, the Buddha taught three linked characteristics of life in the phenomenal world. These three characteristics are Anicca, Anatta, and Dukkha - impermanence, not-self, and stress.

All things in the phenomenal world are subject to impermanence, including what appears as self. All things in the phenomenal world arise and fade away WITHIN the phenomenal world. Nothing is permanent and nothing arises of its own accord.

All things that arise in the phenomenal world are dependent on an infinite number of other impermanent phenomena for existence. This includes what appears to be an individual and eternal self.

The Buddha avoided any attempts to define a self that was contrary to the observable Not-Self characteristic. The Buddha left unanswered any questions that would seek to make permanent and substantial that which is inherently impermanent and insubstantial.

The Buddha never addressed questions directly that would not lead to ending craving and clinging and cessation of dukkha. Answering questions about the nature of self originating from a deluded belief (in self) would only reinforce delusion and lead to more delusion, confusion suffering. These questions were consistently left unanswered as they were improper questions rooted in ignorance.

The Buddha described these questions as arising from "Inappropriate views not fit for attention. These views will continue to generate confusion and suffering."

He teaches what is fit for attention while maintaining the context of The Four Noble Truths: "Understanding Stress, Understanding the Origination of Stress, Understanding the Cessation of Stress, Understanding the path leading to the cessation of Stress. As one attends appropriately in this way, three fetters are abandoned in him: identity-view, doubt, and grasping at precepts & practices." [41]

Grasping at precepts and practices refers to assuming and inherent "ground of being" and engaging in ritualistic practices simply because of the popularity of the doctrine, teacher, or ritual. If engaging or following the doctrine, teacher, or ritual would develop further self-grasping, it should be recognized as deluded and abandoned.

The continued preoccupation with defining and maintaining a self creates ongoing confusion and suffering. Understanding what it is that is perceived to be a self brings liberation.

The Buddha's second discourse, the Anatta-Lakkhana Sutta, or the Sutta on the Not-Self characteristic, teaches that the elements that make up a self are all impermanent. He further teaches that the arising and clinging of these elements all have a cause and that the cause can be recognized and abandoned. Enlightenment in the context of the Second Noble Truth means that the origination of stress and unhappiness, craving and clinging to objects, views, and ideas has been recognized and abandoned.

"Friends, the well-instructed one grows disenchanted with form, disenchanted with feelings, disenchanted with perceptions, disenchanted with fabrications, and disenchanted with thoughts. With

215

disenchantment comes dispassion. With dispassion comes release. With release this one is free and knows 'birth is exhausted, the well-integrated life has been lived, what had to be done has been done, ignorance has ended." [42]

What is being described here is that as a result of whole-hearted engagement with the Eightfold Path disenchantment with the ego-self, with the Five Clinging-Aggregates is developed. From disenchantment with the Five Clinging-Aggregates comes the cessation of the compulsive need to continually establish an ego-personality. Once disenchantment is established the process of unbinding begins. The cessation of delusion, confusion, and continued unsatisfactoriness is now possible.

Dependent Origination

As one develops an understanding of the Dhamma, it is important to always be mindful of the context and intent of the teachings of the Buddha. The Buddha consistently emphasized to be mindful of what he taught and why: "I teach the origination of Dukkha and the cessation of Dukkha, nothing more."

The Buddha avoided any issues that would prove to be a distraction to his stated purpose. In fact, The Buddha could have just as accurately stated "I teach the origination of distraction and the cessation of distraction."

It is the self-referential preoccupation with stress and unhappiness that distracts one from a life of lasting peace and happiness. It is the distraction of dukkha that prevents awakening.

Life in the phenomenal world is often experienced as both arbitrary and personal, and pre-determined and unavoidable. Dependent Origination explains the process of the formation of an ego-personality, a "self," and the personalization of impersonal worldly events. Holding the view that discrete impersonal objects, views and ideas are occurring to "you" or for your benefit or detriment is personalization of impersonal worldly events. This is "I-making."

Recognizing and abandoning the ongoing process of I-making brings the refined mindfulness of an awakened human being. An awakened human being experiences life fully present with life as life occurs without the limiting craving, clinging conditioned mind that clouds perception and maintains confusion and unsatisfactoriness.

Understanding the process of "I-making" develops the heightened wisdom, heightened virtue and heightened concentration necessary to refine thinking and reverse the formation of the ego-personality.

Dependent Origination is the Buddha's teaching on how (apparently) personal phenomena arises within the impersonal environment of impermanence.

The purpose of the Dhamma is to end ignorance through developing profound understanding of The Four Noble Truths. It is within the context of The Four Noble Truths that understanding Dependent Origination develops.

Understanding Dependent Origination brings awareness of the relationship between the five clinging-aggregates and the phenomenal world. The five clinging-aggregates are physical and mental factors that cling together to form a personality identified as self. Dependent Origination explains the 12 causative links that determine the experiences of the ego-personality.

In the Paticca-Samupadda-Vibhanga Sutta the Buddha presents the 12 causative links of dependent Origination. Each of these 12 links are required to cause the "self" to experience confusion, disappointment, sickness, old age, death and rebirth:

"From ignorance as a requisite condition come fabrications.

"From fabrications as a requisite condition comes consciousness.

"From consciousness as a requisite condition comes name-and-form.

"From name-and-form as a requisite condition comes the six sense-base.

"From the six sense-base as a requisite condition comes contact.

"From contact as a requisite condition comes feeling.

"From feeling as a requisite condition comes craving.

"From craving as a requisite condition comes clinging and maintaining.

"From clinging and maintaining as a requisite condition comes becoming.

"From becoming as a requisite condition comes birth.

"From birth as a requisite condition comes aging, sickness, death, sorrow, lamentation, pain, distress and despair." [43]

Then the Buddha describes in slightly more detail, and in reverse order, each of the 12 links:

"Now what is aging and death? Aging is decrepitude, brokenness, graying, decline, weakening of faculties. Death is the passing away of the Five Clinging-Aggregates, the ending of time, the interruption in the life faculties.

"Now what is Birth? Birth is the descent, the coming forth, the coming to be. Birth is the appearance of the six sense-bases and the five clinging-aggregates.

"Now what is becoming? Becoming is sensual becoming, form becoming and formless becoming." [44]

This is explaining that the belief in a self is reinforced by sensory contact and is proliferated by believing in an individual personality being born, i.e.: becoming form. This belief is rooted in ignorance of the Four Noble Truths.

It is also ignorance of The Four Noble Truths to hold the belief that the ego-personality becomes formless at death but survives physical death as the same personality, either in an eternal formless state or being reborn as the same "soul."

Becoming, birth, sickness, old age, death and non-becoming is the environment of dukkha caused by ignorance. The links of clinging, craving, feeling, contact, the six sense-base, name-and-form, consciousness and fabrications are all part of the process of a self arising from ignorance. This process is maintained by continued ignorance, furthering kamma.

Kamma and rebirth is explained in week nine.

The Buddha then describes how clinging to the notion of self maintains this feedback loop of the six-sense base establishing a self and maintaining the cycle of birth, death and rebirth.

"And what is clinging and maintaining? There are four types of clinging: Clinging to sensory stimulus, clinging to views (conditioned thinking), clinging to precepts and practices, and clinging to a doctrine of self." [45]

The Buddha is cautioning against developing or maintaining practices that are given validity simply from the "positive" feeling developed or the "positive" or commonly accepted views reinforced.

Engaging in rituals or practices that continue a doctrine of self in any realm, physical or otherwise are also to be abandoned.

The Buddha here has taken a methodical route from the ultimate unfolding of ignorance, suffering arising from birth (dukkha), back to the second noble truth or the origination of dukkha, craving and clinging. Along the way he describes what is clung to: a self that is dependent on continued craving and continued clinging to sensory stimulus to be maintained.

Profound understanding of any one of these links begins to unravel the entire causative chain.

For example, a profound understanding that phenomena contacting senses develops feelings, and that feeling develops craving (for more self-affirming contact with worldly phenomena) brings dispassion for constant sensory stimulation.

This develops the understanding that contact via sensory stimulus is the direct result of the belief in an ego-self, (name & form) and not an inevitable life experience.

Seeing this process clearly de-personalizes the life experience. From this understanding, life experience no longer will describe and maintain the ego-personality.

The implications of this realization can be unsettling at first if one is engaging the Dhamma to "fix" a flawed self. There is nothing substantial to fix, or to actualize. What is impermanent and insubstantial is to be seen as such, and released.

Remember that what is abandoned when this process of I-making is interrupted is only a fabricated ego-personality that is stuck in confusion and unsatisfactory experiences. Once understood, the release from the burden of an ego-personality brings the continual experience of lasting peace and happiness.

It is also important to remember that the teachings on Dependent Origination are given to develop understanding of The Four Noble Truths. Dependent Origination explains the process of how all personal phenomena arises so that understanding of the distraction of dukkha can be realized. It teaches Right View while pointing out that holding wrong (ignorant) view is the cause of all confusion and suffering.

The emergence of anatta, your ego-personality, within an environment of anicca, resulting in the unsatisfactoriness and confusion of dukkha, is not a personal, arbitrary or chaotic development from which there is no cessation. There is no substantive difference between individual confusion and suffering.

The Four Noble Truths are universal truths applicable to all human experience. Understanding Dependent Origination within the context of The Four Noble Truths is the key to unbinding from the endless kammic entanglements caused by the desire to maintain an ego-self.

Further on in the Paticca-Samupadda-Vibhanga Sutta the Buddha describes how craving arises from feeling, and how feeling is caused by contact.

"And what is craving? There are six classes of craving: craving for forms, craving for sounds, craving for smells, craving for tastes, craving for physical sensations, and craving for ideas.

"And what is feeling? Feeling has six classes as well: feeling arising from eye-contact, from ear-contact-from nose-contact, from taste contact, from body-contact, from intellect-contact. This is called feeling.

"And what is contact? Phenomenon contacting the eye, the ear, the nose, the tongue, the body, and the intellect. This is contact with the six sense-base .

"And what is name and form? Feeling, perception, intention, attention (all mental aspects) and contact. Discriminating consciousness is name. The elements of water, fire, earth and wind, that which makes up physical forms is called forms. Name-and-form is discriminating consciousness bound to, or clinging to, physical form.

"And what is consciousness? There are six classes of consciousness: eye-consciousness, ear-consciousness, nose-consciousness, tongue-consciousness, body-consciousness, intellect-consciousness.

Through the six-sense base contact with the world is made and mental fabrications, including objectifying the self-referential ego-self, is formed.

"And what are fabrications? There are three fabrications: Bodily fabrications, verbal fabrications, and mental fabrications."

All three fabrications are caused by a wrong view of self. Fabrications result in a personality bound to physical form that is perceived as "I" or "me".

The Buddha describes ignorance:

"And what is ignorance? Ignorance is not knowing stress, not knowing the origination of stress, not knowing the cessation of stress, not knowing the (Eightfold) path leading to the cessation of stress. This is called ignorance." [46]

The Buddha relates Dependent Origination back to his first teaching on The Four Noble Truths, and teaches that from ignorance of The Four Noble Truths comes all confusion and suffering.

Gaining understanding of The Four Noble Truths is wisdom. Wisdom brings an end to ignorance and an end to the distraction, confusion and suffering caused by ignorance. Wisdom brings an end to the delusion of an independently arisen self.

When all ignorance is abandoned awakening arises:

"Now from the remainder-less fading & cessation of ignorance comes the cessation of fabrications.

"From the cessation of fabrications comes the cessation of consciousness.

"From the cessation of consciousness comes the cessation of name-and-form.

"From the cessation of name-and-form comes the cessation of the six sense-base.

"From the cessation of the six sense-base comes the cessation of contact.

"From the cessation of contact comes the cessation of feeling.

"From the cessation of feeling comes the cessation of craving.

"From the cessation of craving comes the cessation of clinging and maintaining.

"From the cessation of clinging and maintaining comes the cessation of becoming.

"From the cessation of becoming comes the cessation of birth.

"From the cessation of birth comes the cessation of sickness, aging, death, sorrow, pain, distress, despair and confusion. Wisdom brings the cessation to the entire mass of stress and suffering." [47]

The Eightfold Path is a path that develops heightened wisdom, heightened virtue and heightened concentration. All three qualities of mind are requisite conditions to end ignorance. Developing these three qualities creates the condition for the cessation of ignorance.

Dependent Origination describes the ongoing process rooted in ignorance that fabricates the ego-personality and how the ego-personality, how anatta, is maintained by craving and clinging. This is perhaps the most significant difference between the Buddha's teachings and religious and philosophical systems, including most later-developed Buddhist schools.

A modern example of this is the misunderstanding and misapplication of Dependent Origination used to develop a doctrine of interdependence, interconnectedness, and inter-being between individual and insubstantial ego-personality's. As noted in the previous chapter these doctrines only encourage and maintain craving and clinging.

All human beings are connected through the common problem of delusion and suffering. This is described as The First Noble Truth. Creating something more of this simple fact leads to contradictory and confusing doctrines that perpetuate continued "I-making."

Notice that there is no actual beginning in time nor birth of a "soul" or any individual entity. The process of becoming an ego-self begins in ignorance, produces delusion and suffering, and (the process) can be brought to cessation through wisdom and understanding.

Having arisen from ignorance, only continued ignorance can sustain ignorance and perpetuate dukkha. Wrong views are formed and deluded beliefs created to provide substance to what is inherently insubstantial.

Dependent Origination shows that from a wrong or ignorant view the manifestation of an ego-personality is fabricated. Fabricated, the process of continued fabrication can be brought to an end.

It is within an impermanent environment that a sense-based consciousness arises. Here stress arises as consciousness continually struggles to maintain a permanent and substantial view of self. With each passing moment, in every instant, all things pass away and all things are reborn.

It requires constant vigilance and continual fabrication to maintain the establishment of an ego-self. It is the stress of maintaining wrong views that distracts from recognizing the mirage-like nature of these views.

Through understanding Dependent Origination it is seen that clinging to a view of self occurs. Keeping this self comfortable, safe, engaged and most importantly continually established, then becomes the sole purpose for existence. This is continual distraction. This is dukkha.

The Eightfold Path provides the framework and Right View, or right perspective, for observing and interrupting Dependent Origination. In order to see this process clearly any notion if "I" or "me" being the cause of Dependent Origination, of being the ignorant individual that begins the process must be abandoned.

Here is a seeming paradox: The ongoing ignorance of an ego-self must be recognized and abandoned through the development of wisdom. It is also wrong view to conclude that it is an ego-self that is gaining wisdom. There is nothing substantial or sustainable to gain wisdom. The views of an ego-self are rooted in ignorance. Ignorance can never give rise to wisdom, to understanding. Wisdom arises when ignorance of the Four Noble Truths is supplanted by the profound knowledge of stress, and the experience of cessation of The Five Clinging-Aggregates.

The developed skills of concentration and mindfulness and the ongoing direction and guidance of the Eightfold Path diminishes "I-making" or conceit. It is from this perspective that Dependent Origination can be usefully and effectively understood.

The Buddha was asked on one occasion "is the one who acts the same one who experiences the result of an act?" (Notice the self-identification in the question)

The Buddha responds "To say the one who acts is the one who experiences is one extreme. To say the one who acts is someone other than the one who experiences is the other extreme." (This is the belief in outside forces such as creation, reward, or punishment bringing individual experiences.)

The Buddha continues: "I teach the Dhamma from the middle, a middle way. I avoid those extreme views and teach that from (individual) ignorance brings all manner of delusion and suffering. Whoever declares that pleasure and pain are self made, whoever declares that pleasure and pain are other made, are deluded. All experiences are dependent on contact and contact is (initially) dependent on ignorance." [48]

This brings up another contradictory teaching of later-developed Buddhist schools that misunderstand or misapply Dependent Origination. The ego-self, anatta, has no inherent nature. There is no Buddhahood or Buddha-nature for the ego-self to aspire to. This doctrine creates confusion and further establishment of the ego-self. If there is an inner Buddhahood or Buddha-nature how could it succumb to ignorance? These are simply deluded doctrines rooted in ignorance.

It is the ego-self that has no substantial nature. Developing understanding of what is perceived to be an ego-self is paramount so that all attempts at continuing to establish anatta are abandoned.

There is nothing in the Buddha's teachings that support the notion of an inner Buddha-nature. Once awakened a human being is free of craving, clinging, delusion and ongoing suffering. This includes clinging the ego-self to an imaginary idea of an inner, obscure Buddha-nature.

This is what the Buddha taught. Being free of all clinging views is lasting peace and happiness. This is enough!

To reiterate, I am not disparaging later-developed teachings. I am providing clarity as to what the Buddha taught and in the context that he presented his Dhamma.

In the Simsapa Sutta the Buddha explains the refined purpose of the Dhamma: "And what have I taught? 'I teach the nature of dukkha (stress). I teach the origination of dukkha (craving and clinging originate dukkha). I teach that cessation of dukkha is possible. I teach that The Eightfold Path is the path leading to the cessation of dukkha: This is what I have taught. " [49] (Repeated here for emphasis.)

The Buddha describes the insubstantiality of the mental/physical form in the Dhammapada, v.46 as "Having known this body likened unto foam and understanding thoroughly its nature is mirage-like."
[50]

Dependent Origination shows that continued confusion and suffering is dependent on continued ignorance. Dukkha originates in a series of 12 "dependencies" rooted in ignorance. Developing wisdom and understanding through the Eightfold Path brings an end to ignorance.

Shamatha-Vipassana meditation is very effective in interrupting the compulsion to continually maintain ignorance and the establishment of an ego-personality. Mindfulness of the breath settles the mind and develops deep and useful concentration. As distraction lessens and non-distraction develops it becomes possible to observe Dependent Origination as it occurs. True insight is insight into the formation of self-referential, ego-self-sustaining views, arising from ignorance.

Aversion to the Dhamma often arises as the Dhamma points directly to seeing clearly the insubstantial nature of self. All manner of adaptations and accommodations have been made to the Buddha's original teachings to avoid this aversion. These general hindrances were discussed in chapter two. Hindrances arise from the ego-personality's need to continually establish and maintain its existence in every object, view, and idea that occurs.

Hindrances to maintaining a Dhamma practice is explained in week ten.

Of course, it is the fabricated ego-personality's obsession with maintaining views that is put aside through the Eightfold Path. This is often experienced like annihilation because it is. It is annihilation of all that would continue delusion, confusion, unsatisfactoriness, and suffering. Awakening is abandoning all views of self that have arisen from ignorance.

As seen through understanding Dependent Origination, clinging and craving are necessary if an ego-self is to be established and maintained. Clinging and craving subsides by remaining mindful of the Eightfold Path. As clinging and craving subside, concentration develops and deepens. As concentration deepens, the distraction caused by ignorance ends and wisdom arises.

Awakening occurs through developing a profound understanding of the underlying unsatisfactory nature of life within the moral, ethical and concentrative framework of The Eightfold Path.

Through ignorance as the cause, the conditions of distraction, confusion and suffering occur. Through wisdom as the cause, the condition of awakening occurs. The Eightfold Path is a path of virtue and concentration which develops perfect wisdom.

Dependent Origination describes the impersonal process resulting in confusion and suffering founded in ignorance. The Five Clinging-Aggregates describe the impersonal nature of the perception of an individual, permanent, personal self. Remember that the Dhamma is taught in the context of the Four Noble Truths. The Five

Clinging Aggregates do not seek to explain a "self." The Five Clinging-Aggregates describe the clinging vehicle that experiences suffering. When viewed from this Right View, The Five Clinging Aggregates are anatta, not-self, anicca, impermanent, and so dukkha. The Five Clinging Aggregates are also known as the Five Kandhas.

The Five Clinging-Aggregates, The Five Kandhas

"Clinging has craving as its cause. Craving is dependent on feelings, feelings dependent on contact. Contact is dependent on the six-sense base and the six-sense base dependent on the establishment of an ego-personality. The ego-personality is dependent on consciousness, consciousness dependent on fabrications. And what is the root of fabrications and the entire mass of confusion and suffering? Fabrications (deluded thinking) are dependent on ignorance for it's cause.

From the cessation of ignorance comes true insight and the cessation of fabrications. From true insight comes cessation of clinging to sensory stimulus, to views and ideas, to rituals and practices or doctrines of self. This wise one is free of clinging, unbound, at peace. Being at peace they know 'confusion and stress have ended. The integrated life has been lived. All tasks have been completed. There is nothing further for this world." [51]

The Five Aggregates

Form, matter (Pali: Rupa) The physical body and the physical domain. Included in the physical body are the senses and the thinking conditioned mind. The physical or phenomenal domain is all that we perceive through contact with the senses. Any physical form is called the form aggregate.

Feeling (Pali: Vedana) Feeling is the experienced reaction to mental or physical stimulus. Any emotional or physical feeling is called the feeling aggregate.

Perception (Pali: Sanna) Perceptions are views formed by discriminating thoughts. Reaction to

237

perceptions further integrates the perception and further conditions the mind. Perception bound to a false view of self results in a deluded view of reality. It is through perception that we convey permanent and individuated reality where none exists. Delusion arises by believing that simply because we think something is as it appears to be, it is. This is discursive thinking, much like "I think therefore I am." This is also mental/physical sleight-of hand you are the magician. Any perception is called the perception aggregate.

Mental Fabrications (Pali: Sankhara) Mental fabrications are thought constructs and held views. Mental fabrications develop from sensory stimulus perceived through wrong view, further conditioning clinging conditioned mind. Mental fabrications incline your mind to wrong views creating unskillful actions. It is unskillful volitional actions originating in deluded intentions that cause kamma. Sankhara is a component of consciousness. Any mental fabrication is called the fabrication aggregate.

Consciousness (Pali: Vinana) That which arises within form due to contact with the six senses (Sadayatana, five physical senses and thought). This is not to be taken as a part of an awakened mind.

Consciousness bound to the clinging-aggregates is also impermanent. Consciousness is the active and reactive process of an ego-personality continually establishing itself. Any aspect of consciousness is called the consciousness aggregate.

Notice the close relationship between the five aggregates and the causative links of Dependent Origination. The aggregate of form relates to the last eight "links" of Dependent Origination. The aggregate of feeling is the requisite condition for craving (and indirectly relates to name & form, the six-sense base and contact.) The aggregate of perception relates to fabrications as does consciousness.

The aggregate of form originates in ignorance and is animated by consciousness and results in name & form.

The aggregate of feeling originates in ignorance and is animated by contact with your six-sense base and results in craving.

The aggregate of perception originates in ignorance and is animated by feelings consciousness.

The Aggregate of mental Fabrications originates in ignorance and results in (deluded) consciousness.

239

The Aggregate of consciousness originates in ignorance and is animated by mental fabrications resulting in the experience of confusion and unsatisfactoriness.

The significance of this is to understand that the Five Clinging-Aggregates are dependent on ignorance. End ignorance and the vehicle for continued confusion and suffering unbinds and unravels. Penetrating (complete understanding) the Five Clinging-Aggregates, or any single component of Dependent Origination, begins to unravel clinging and bring an end to ignorance.

When any aggregate binds to any other element through clinging it is called a clinging-aggregate. It is through these aggregates of observable phenomenon that a perception of a self arises. For example: when a physical form binds to a mental fabrication called John it is now a clinging-aggregate. John has a pleasant (or unpleasant) experience. Perception evaluates the feeling and further conditions consciousness to crave more (or less) of the experience.

Life becomes an endless experience of sensory input followed by discrimination. Each experience is filtered through discriminating and conditioned thought. Each experience provides more validity to the arisen form and further conditioning the consciousness of the form.

Notice that each of these factors is impermanent and uncertain. Through unskillful and deluded intention to establish a self based on these five impermanent factors your ego-personality is formed. From a wrong, or ignorant view, your ego-personality is established. Due to clinging to objects, ideas, and views your ego-personality is defended and maintained. It is your ego-personality, or not-self, that is subject to unsatisfactoriness, unhappiness, disappointment, stress and suffering.

Being mindful of the Right Intention to recognize and abandon craving and clinging begins to unbind the five clinging-aggregates. Dependent Origination shows that it is from the condition of craving that the condition of clinging arises. Understanding the five clinging-aggregates begins to unbind the aggregates and brings the refined mindfulness to see the individual components for what they are and to (eventually) abandon the need to continue the ego-self through continued clinging.

The Buddha is using the concept of the five clinging-aggregates to show the insubstantial and impermanent nature of what is perceived as an individual:

"The five aggregates are anicca, impermanent; whatever is impermanent, that is dukkha, unsatisfactory; whatever is dukkha, that is without self. What is without self, that is not mine, that I am not, that is not my self. Thus should it be seen by perfect wisdom as it really is. Who sees by perfect wisdom, as it really is, his mind, not grasping, is detached from fabrications; he is liberated." [52]

The Eightfold Path provides the framework for developing mindfulness and concentration. Mindfulness and concentration brings insight into the truth of the Five Clinging-Aggregates giving rise to the appearance of a self. Upon investigation it becomes clear that these aggregates are impermanent manifestations of mental and physical phenomenon given substance by conditioned thinking.

What we perceive as an individual self is a mental/physical personality that has arisen from conditioned mind by ignorance. Individuality or an individual personality should be understood as a combination, or an aggregate, of phenomena. The desire for an individual and permanent form is the cause of suffering. This is craving for existence.

All conditioned thoughts and fabrications arise from this initial thirst. The concept of a substantial and eternal self endowed with a soul arises from craving for existence. Acquiring a view of a soul brings a belief of eternity to the temporary phenomenon of the ego-personality, or not-self, continuing delusion and suffering.

The skillful view here is to not get too analytical as analysis does not develop insight. It is enough to recognize that by phenomenal contact with your six-sense base reaction occurs and is interpreted by the four aspects of consciousness. The Five Clinging-Aggregates experience this reaction and a personality is affirmed and established.

Reaction to sensory stimulus seems to give an experience validity. The experience is only "validated' within the impermanence of the Five Clinging-Aggregates. Initial reaction to the implications of the truth of the Five Clinging-Aggregates can be disconcerting at first. Conditioned mind will reject any thought that self is without any permanent substance.

Understanding the Five Clinging-Aggregates does not limit or annihilate anything of actual substance. Understanding the Five Clinging-

243

Aggregates shines the light of wisdom on the darkness of ignorance. Understanding frees your limited view of self that is bound to an impermanent and insubstantial "heap" of phenomenal elements.

The insistence on maintaining the delusion that an individual self is anything more than these Five Clinging-Aggregates continues to give rise to dukkha. It is the constant preoccupation with the distraction of dukkha that obscures wisdom.

Abandoning craving for existence and clinging to form is enlightenment. The distraction of the preoccupation with dukkha is lifted and Awakened Right View arises.

The Four Noble Truths explains the truth of stress, its origins, and the path leading to the cessation of stress. The Five Clinging-Aggregates explains the process that leads to the belief in an individual self subject to The Four Noble Truths. Anicca, Dukkha, and Anatta explains the environment that the appearance of self and The Four Noble Truths are a part of.

Due to impermanence the Buddha teaches: "Form is not-self, feelings are not self, perception is not self, mental fabrications are not self, and consciousness is not self."

The five factors, or aggregates, of form, feelings, perceptions, mental fabrications, and consciousness combine to give the appearance of a "self."

When personalized through self-identification these five factors are now self-referential clinging components of "myself." With refined mindfulness, these five elements can be clearly seen as five separate elements.

Creating a personal and permanent self-identity from impersonal and impermanent factors results in a deluded view. The Buddha described this deluded view as "Anatta." As seen in the previous chapter, Anatta means "Not-A-Self." The Buddha is teaching that what is commonly viewed as a self, as "atta," due to the delusion seemingly validated by The Five Clinging-Aggregates, is in fact Anatta, Not-A-Self.

You create self-establishing and self-referential views by identifying as a form that is animated by sensory input. The sensory input develops feelings. You decide if what has contacted your senses enhances, diminishes, or is neutral in effect to what is now established as "you."

This feedback loop now continually affirms the belief that your form is in fact substantial and permanent. This belief is based solely on feedback from your six sense-base.

Notice how this process is rooted in the ignorant belief that a temporary form animated by temporary and arbitrary sense impressions must in fact be an individual. This is wrong view. This is discursive thinking. This is using an ignorant view to validate ongoing ignorant views based on the same feedback that set the deluded experience unfolding.

Do you see how ongoing ignorance is required to further this deluded thinking? Do you see how the inclination to ignore what would bring wisdom is an underlying factor of ignorance?

The Five Clinging-Aggregates refer to the appearance of a "self" that craves for existence and clings to what seems too establish "self-existence." This process originates and perpetuate delusion, confusion and ongoing unsatisfactoriness.

The Four Noble Truths do not refer to an individual "self" that experiences the unsatisfactory nature of life in a personal way. The Four Noble Truths do not establish an individual "self" that originates craving and clinging.

The Four Noble Truths are universal and impersonal truths that all human beings are subject to:

1. There is confusion, delusion, unsatisfactoriness. There is Dukkha.

2. Craving and Clinging originates and perpetuates confusion, delusion, unsatisfactoriness.

3. Cessation of confusion, delusion, unsatisfactoriness is possible.

4. The path to cessation of confusion, delusion, unsatisfactoriness is the Eightfold Path.

Notice that there is no permanent "self" that is referenced. These are statements of the truth of existence in this world.

The teaching of the Five Clinging-Aggregates is a simple and practical explanation of the personalization of impersonal phenomena.

The Five Clinging-Aggregates do not describe an established self in an absolute sense. The Five Clinging-Aggregates describe in a relative sense, in the context of The Four Noble Truths, and relative to worldly phenomena, the manifestation of dukkha.

Once the process of Dependent Origination "originates" from wrong or ignorant view (ignorant of The Four Noble Truths) kamma then must provide an expressive manifestation of ignorance. The Five Clinging-Aggregates is an impermanent and impersonal manifestation originating in ignorance.

Kamma is a word that describes the ongoing process of Dukkha. Kamma means action. It is past intentional actions moderated by present mindfulness that results in current experience, or present Kamma. Kamma and Rebirth is explained fully in week nine.

The Five Clinging-Aggregates describe the illusion of a permanent self providing the understanding to bring to cessation the ongoing attempt to continue to establish a "self."

Once it is clearly seen that these five components are insubstantial and dependent on ignorance to maintain, and prone to constant unsatisfactory experiences, self-referential thoughts and fabrications will be abandoned.

In the language of the Buddha, "Kandha" had many meanings: Heap, pile, mass, a trunk of a tree. Nibbana, final release from craving and clinging, is described as "extinguishing the fires of passion" and relates to the burning away of a tree trunk. Also, as will be seen, Heap, pile, and mass also help describe the Five Clinging-Aggregates. The Buddha, as he often did, used common terms (of his day) to explain the Dhamma.

The Five Clinging-Aggregates explains that from ignorance a deluded view is formed. This ignorant view obscures reality and creates distraction. This results in the combining of five disparate parts, or aggregates, to objectify and provide a vehicle for the ensuing confusion and suffering.

This is a key concept of the Dhamma. If this is unclear at this point, remember that the Eightfold Path develops the wisdom and understanding to see this reality clearly.

From the point of view of an ego-personality this often sounds like nonsense. Resistance to seeing clearly, to useful insight, is rooted in wrong view. An aspect of ignorance is the ego-personality's inclination to ignore anything that would challenge its existence.

When faced with truths that would bring wisdom to the ignorance that the ego-self is dependent on for continuance, questions such as "what am I?" and "what happens to me?" arise. (when I awaken, when I die, etc.) These questions seek answers that would continue to establish the Five Clinging-Aggregates.

These are inappropriate questions as they are rooted in the ignorance of the ego-self. Continued ignorance can not diminish ignorance. Clinging to views that have arisen from ignorance will only further ignorance and the ensuing confusion and suffering.

The Buddha consistently refused to answer self-referential questions, often replying "I teach suffering and the cessation of suffering. I teach The Four Noble Truths, nothing more."

The Buddha was also cautious in discussing any mental fabrications that would likely generate more confusion and stress.

The wanderer Vacchagotta had many questions about the nature of the cosmos, eternity, infinitude, the self and the soul, existence after death, and others. After he put these questions to the Buddha, the Buddha responded: "You are confused (by your own questions). The phenomenon (Dependent Origination) you question is hard to understand realize. This phenomenon is tranquil and subtle and beyond discriminating thought. Realization only comes to the awakened." [53]

The Five Clinging-Aggregates are taught to develop the understanding of suffering, not to describe and establish a self.

Understanding the Five Clinging-Aggregates within the context of this course and within the context of The Four Noble Truths begins to diminish attachment to these ignorant views allowing for wisdom and Right View to arise.

Anicca, impermanence, shows that what is perceived of as a substantial and eternal self is in truth insubstantial and impermanent. Being impermanent, the ego-self is subject to stress and unhappiness due to craving and clinging to views of a permanent and substantial self.

It is ignorance that brings suffering. It is the belief in an individual soul or personality that provides the vehicle for the establishment and continuation of suffering. It is the constant preoccupation and distraction of dukkha that obscures liberation and freedom. One can't know what is not known until what is believed to be true is abandoned. Insisting on maintaining the delusion of an individual self is a wrong view that is blocking Right View.

Understanding the Five Clinging-Aggregates does not answer the question of "what am I?" Understanding the Five Clinging-Aggregates brings wisdom to the nature of suffering.

Next week's study will develop understanding of kamma and rebirth. Kamma and rebirth explains the condition caused by the ongoing unfolding of delusional beliefs. Through intention and volitional acts arising from a lack of understanding a self that suffers is maintained. Liberation arises and the mind awakens once all deluded views are abandoned:

"When ignorance is abandoned and true knowledge has arisen one no longer clings to sensual pleasures. One no longer clings to views, or to rules and observances, or to a doctrine of self. When one does not cling, one is not agitated. When one is not agitated, one attains Nibbana. Wisdom arises and birth is left behind. The life of virtue, mindful concentration and wisdom has been lived. The righteous Eightfold Path has been developed. There will be no more becoming to any state of being." [54]

The Buddha's teachings are not to be only studied intellectually. The Buddha's teachings are to be understood through wisdom born of the experience of integrating these teachings into your life.

Observe the Five Clinging-Aggregates and how they give rise to a belief in self. Notice that nothing arises without clinging, craving or desire. Notice the unskillful intention to acquire or to become. Notice how the belief in the self continues the discursive cycle of craving, acquisition, disappointment and more craving.

This is also a practical lesson in Dependent Origination. The root craving for existence gives rise to a self that clings. The self is dependent on clinging for existence, and on continued craving to maintain existence. Clinging to the notion of a separate and individual self lessens by developing understanding through The Eightfold Path.

The Eightfold Path is the practical and direct way of understanding The Four Noble Truths and the belief in a self within the environment of Anicca. Wisdom and understanding arise and the idea of an individual self is abandoned. There is no more becoming as there is nothing for desire to arise from. The veil of dukkha is lifted.

While meditating with tranquility, allow insight to arise and have a direct experience of the Buddha's teachings leading to abandoning clinging and the cessation of suffering. Experience awakening through unbinding the Five Clinging-Aggregates.

"Magandiya, when you hear the true Dhamma, you will practice the Dhamma correctly. When you practice the Dhamma correctly, you will know & see for yourself: 'This is where confusion and suffering ceases without trace. With the cessation of my clinging comes the cessation of becoming. With the cessation of becoming comes the cessation of birth. With the cessation of birth then aging & death, sorrow, lamentation, pain, distress, & despair all cease. Such is the cessation of this entire mass of suffering & stress." [55]

The Buddha describes a mind free of clinging and freed of association to the five clinging aggregates: "released from clinging the mind is without feature or surface, limitless, outside of time and space, freed from the six-sense base." [56]

This Week's Dhamma Study

- Listen to the week eight talk on Understanding Not-Self:
  http://crossrivermeditation.com/truth-of-happiness-online-course-talks/

- Continue with your meditation practice in the morning and early evening. If you feel comfortable with adding a few minutes to your practice do so. Ten to twenty minute meditation sessions should be comfortable for you.

- In meditation, remain mindful of your breathing as you dispassionately notice feelings and thoughts arise and dissipate. When you notice that you are caught up in your own thoughts and have lost awareness of your breath, put aside the focus on your thoughts and place your awareness on your breathing. Become aware of your mind from a dispassionate observational view, a mind-state of choiceless awareness always mindful of your breath.

- At the end of your meditation sessions take a moment to notice the quality of your mind. Be at peace with the quality of your mind.

- Continue to develop wisdom by noticing your attachments to the people and events of your life, including yourself. Continue to generate the Right Intention to let go of all attachments and all impermanent views.

- In your day-to-day life notice when you are engaged in Right Speech, Action and Livelihood and when you are not. Continue to develop the strong intention to abandon all wrong speech, action and livelihood. As concentration deepens, non-virtuous thoughts, words and deeds become apparent.

- Continue to develop Right Effort. Put aside time for a regular meditation practice and maintain a priority to your practice. There will always be life events distracting away from practice. Very rarely will these events be more immediate or important than putting aside some time twice a day for a period of meditation. Bring mindfulness into all areas of your life by staying focused in the present moment.

- Notice any persistent thoughts and your awareness of the impermanence of all thoughts. Avoid being analytical. This is a dispassionate observance of thoughts and feelings as they arise and pass away. Take note of developing a more mindful presence in your life. Notice when you are fully present with another. Notice when you are not as distracted or reactive.

- Continue your Dhamma study with week nine.

- Always be gentle with yourself and enjoy your practice!

If taking the correspondence course:

- Write a paragraph or two regarding your Dhamma practice and write down any questions or insights into impermanence and how impermanence contributes to stress and unhappiness. Note your deepening understanding of how impermanence and clinging give rise to the stress and unhappiness of the ego-personality.

- Write an additional paragraph or two regarding your understanding of the Five Clinging-Aggregates and Dependent Origination and how these teachings explain the formation of an ego-personality and the environment that gives rise to non-self.

- To submit your writing, please use this form: http://crossrivermeditation.com/home-study-submissions/

- I will respond to you within 24 to 48 hours.

Week Nine
Kamma and Rebirth

"I am the owner of my actions, heir to my actions. I am born of my actions and related through my actions. My actions will determine the fortune or misfortune in my life." [57]

Kamma (Sanskrit: Karma) and Rebirth are closely linked concepts of the Buddha's teachings. Despite modern presentations that the Buddha taught kamma and rebirth only to relate to the prevalent beliefs of his time and are not useful or relevant teachings, understanding kamma and rebirth is essential to these teachings.

The Buddha's teachings on kamma and rebirth refuted many of the common beliefs of his time and helped clarify the purpose and experience of awakening. Understanding these teachings as they were originally presented and in the context of The Four Noble Truths brings insight and clarity to the Eightfold Path and can help one recognize contradictory and confusing "Buddhist" teachings that are later-developed adaptations and accommodations to the original teachings.

Kamma and Rebirth are conditions arising from ignorance. Kamma means action. Kamma is in no way punishment as a result of arbitrary judgments from a supreme being. Kamma is not the consequences from a vague independent moral-ethical-spiritual system.

Kamma is not a condition imposed on you. You alone are the cause of your kamma and you alone are the cause of rebirth.

Kamma should not be viewed simply as what is unfolding in your life. Kamma is the present unfolding of past intentional actions moderated by your present state of understanding and quality of mindfulness. As your present state of mindfulness and understanding animate your current actions, your current actions are moderating the effects of past actions.

What this means is the key to these entire teachings. Through mindfulness imbued with wisdom and motivated by Right Intention, the unfolding of kamma can be inclined towards release and awakening. Developing understanding of the process rooted in ignorance resulting in confusion and suffering brings the ability to end ignorance with profound wisdom. By understanding the process you can reverse the process.

Kamma does not pre-determine life. Mindful and well-concentrated intention within the framework of the Eightfold Path develops release from craving and clinging and cessation of suffering.

"Whatever one continues to pursue with their thinking becomes the inclination of their awareness. Being mindful of Right Intention and abandoning thinking imbued with craving, clinging, and sensuality inclines the mind towards release." [58]

All of the events of life are not the result of individual kamma. Most of what occurs in one's life is simply worldly conditions and described in the First Noble Truth: "There is stress." Reaction to impersonal events will create additional kamma and further conditions mind.

Reaction arises from wrong views of self and it is wrong views that initiate and proliferate kamma. Once all wrong views of self are abandoned the establishment of further kamma ends.

As with all the Buddha's original teachings, kamma is taught in the context of The Four Noble Truths with the goal of the cessation of suffering. In this context, kamma describes the ongoing suffering rooted in ignorance and reinforced by wrong intention.

"Kamma should be understood (correctly). The cause of kamma should be understood. The diversity (of the results) of kamma should be understood. Cessation of kamma should be understood. The path developing the cessation of kamma should be understood. " [59]

Notice that these are the same words the Buddha uses to describe the truth of suffering. Kamma unfolding, whether experienced as pleasure or pain, is an aspect of dukkha and originates in craving and clinging. This brings Dependent Origination (ignorance resulting in suffering) and Right Intention into understanding and ending kamma.

The Buddha continues: "Intention is kamma. With intention one does kamma through thought, word, and deed. And what is the cause that initiates kamma? Contact."

This again relates to Dependent Origination and the importance of unraveling the links of Dependent Origination. Through Right Intention supported by the other seven factors of the Eightfold Path the ongoing process of ignorance resulting in confusion and suffering can be brought to an end through wisdom and ensuing right actions (again, kamma means action).

The Buddha continues: "And what is the cessation of kamma? From the cessation of contact comes the cessation of kamma. And how does one experience the cessation of contact? Through the Noble Eightfold Path."

This shows that the driving force to continue confusion and suffering is described by the Buddha as kamma. This is to point out the importance of being mindful of all thoughts, words, and deeds. This is the purpose of mindfulness in the context of The Four Noble Truths. It is your actions that will determine your awakening or continued confusion and suffering. The framework for recognizing, understanding, and refining your actions is the Eightfold Path.

Through whole-hearted engagement with the Eightfold Path you are taking actions that directly influence the unfolding of your kamma and incline your kamma towards developing a life of lasting peace and happiness.

Kamma is your ego-personality's experience of craving and clinging within anicca. Kamma is the direct experience of the results of ignorance. Understanding kamma is understanding dukkha. Understanding dukkha inclines your mind towards abandoning craving and clinging and begins to unravel the links of Dependent Origination.

With awakened Right View no attachment to the ego-personality is present and any experience is simply an experience in the world that is dispassionately observed with mindful presence.

Any event that occurs in the phenomenal world is an opportunity to remain dispassionately present with a mind settled in equanimity and to cease creating additional kamma. Once a reaction to an event has occurred, further kamma is established. A mind settled in equanimity will cease creating additional kamma.

"A fool and a wise person are both characterized by their actions. It is through the actions of one's life that reveals the fool or the sage. The fool engages in three things: bodily misconduct, verbal misconduct, and mental misconduct. The sage engages in three things: good bodily conduct, good verbal conduct, and good mental conduct.

"Thus friends, train yourselves as a sage in thought, word, and deed." [60]

Your experience of the unfolding of your kamma is not pre-determined. The state or quality of your mind in each moment determines your experience of kamma unfolding. A reactive mind will further kamma. A mind of equanimity will bring a peaceful experience of kamma unfolding and avoid additional kamma.

While it is more desirable to experience the effects of kamma pleasurably, to have "good kamma," all kamma contributes to dukkha and rebirth. All kamma is to be extinguished.

Holding the conscious intention to act in a certain manner to develop favorable kamma will accomplish just that: develop additional kamma. The result will be to forever perpetuate dukkha. This is why it is crucial to be mindful of Right View and the strong resolve, the Right Intention, to abandon all craving and clinging, and awaken.

Dukkha describes the underlying unsatisfactory experience of life in the phenomenal world. Kamma describes your contribution to your experience of the underlying unsatisfactory experience. Your kamma is your dukkha. Your intentional actions will result in the continuation or cessation of confusion and stress.

Altruistic or compassionate actions taken without wisdom can often generate further kammic entanglements. This can be very subtle and difficult to recognize. For example, if an underlying motivation and intention for compassionate action is to fulfill a view of what it means to be a "good " person, even a "good Buddhist," the resulting kamma will be reinforcing your ego-personality.

Altruistic and compassionate actions that are an expression of an enlightened mind will always benefit all with no kammic entanglements or consequences.

This is not to say that one should not act with compassion and in accordance with the framework of the Eightfold Path. The Eightfold Path provides guidance against continued self-identification and continued "I-making."

Holding the intention to establish and defend an ego-self leads to action and reaction that inevitably creates additional kamma.

Holding in mind the intention to recognize and abandon craving and clinging will incline kamma towards release. The life experience will naturally be more peaceful and meaningful.

Kamma is the experience of self in this present moment. Who you see yourself to be is the result of kamma or past actions unfolding in the present state of your mindfulness.

Kamma is who you are in this moment in the phenomenal world. The more skillful your actions in the present, the more liberating will be your kamma as life unfolds. Mindfulness of the Eightfold Path inclines you to Right Action.

By being mindful of the Dhamma and living with the integrity that arises from following The Eightfold Path, you directly impact kamma in the present moment. You will change the direction of your life by changing your intentional actions and reactions.

The Eightfold Path is the framework for clearly seeing your actions, reactions, and unfolding kamma. Your actions and reactions change as your thoughts become virtuous, your mind becomes less distracted, and wisdom deepens.

Holding the intention to abandon all clinging, craving, desire and aversion diminishes the distraction of dukkha. Abandoning clinging interrupts the ongoing establishment and defense of your ego-self.

Unskillful intentions and resulting actions will create additional kamma. Right Intention will lead to cessation of unskillful actions and bringing an end to kamma.

Right Intention is holding the strong resolve to put aside all clinging, craving, desire and aversion. Right Intention arising from Right View generates the moral and ethical actions of Right Speech, Action and Livelihood. The virtuous aspects of The Eightfold Path lead to the abandonment of desire. Right Intention arising from Right View informs a practice developing Right Effort, Right Mindfulness and Right Meditation.

At Savatthi the Buddha said: "Monks, what a person wills, what they plan, what they dwell on forms the basis for the continuation of consciousness. This basis being present, consciousness has a lodgment. Consciousness being lodged there and growing, rebirth of renewed existence takes place in the future, and from this renewed existence arise birth, decay-and-death, grief, lamentation, suffering, sorrow and despair. Such is the uprising of this entire mass of suffering.

"Even if a person does not will and plan, yet if they dwell on something this forms a basis for the continuation of consciousness:... rebirth... takes place...

"But if a person neither wills nor plans nor dwells on anything, no basis is formed for the continuation of consciousness. This basis being absent, consciousness has no lodgment. Consciousness not being lodged there and not growing, no rebirth of renewed existence takes place in the future, and so birth, decay-and-death, grief, lamentation, suffering, sorrow and despair are destroyed. Such is the cessation of this entire mass of suffering." [61]

Notice how this last passage relates to Dependent Origination. Remember that all of these teachings are to develop understanding of confusion

269

and suffering and the cessation of future confusion and suffering. By gaining wisdom one no longer acts from ignorance. With no ignorance there is no basis for the establishment of mental fabrications or discriminating and discursive consciousness. With no consciousness established there is nothing to sustain the Five Clinging-Aggregates. With no sustenance, the 12 Links of Dependent Origination un-bind. With no sustenance, a moment free of delusion, confusion, and unsatisfactoriness, a moment free of dukkha is born.

There will be no more births rooted in ignorance and subject to endless confusion and suffering. Lasting peace and happiness has been established through the Eightfold Path.

Unlike most religions, and many modern "Buddhist" religions, acting to gain favorable future experiences post physical death is contrary to the Dhamma. As has been seen, birth is the beginning of the experience of the "whole mass of suffering." As confusion and unsatisfactoriness is the underlying pervasive experience of life in the phenomenal world, the ending of kamma and the cessation of future births is the purpose of the Dhamma.

An awakened mind settled in equanimity will produce no additional kamma. As no additional kamma is created, residual kamma will simply ripen and fall away until complete liberation and freedom is realized.

The following three paragraphs bring previously developed teachings into the context of kamma and rebirth.

The three defining characteristics of the phenomenal world are Anicca, Dukkha and Anatta. Within the environment of impermanence Dukkha arises. Dukkha arises due to clinging, craving and aversion. Clinging arises from a misunderstanding of the nature of self.

What arises as "self" (shown to be anatta, not a self) is an impermanent combination of factors known as "The Five Clinging-Aggregates. These aggregates are described as clinging due to the nature of "self" to cling to thoughts, ideas, and objects that further define and describe self. It is craving and clinging rooted in ignorance that establishes a self and creates Kamma and the cycles of birth.

Anatta or "not-self" refers to the impermanent nature of the formation of a self that is subject to stress, disappointment and confusion.

271

The Buddha never taught that there is a self or that there is not a self. He avoided the issue as a focus on metaphysical questions would be a distraction from his stated purpose to bring "an understanding of dukkha and a cessation of dukkha. Nothing more."

He taught that what is commonly believed to be a self is not founded in Right Understanding. It is this conditioned view of self that is to be abandoned if confusion and suffering is to end.

As the distraction of dukkha is always present to a deluded mind, then the awakened mind is a mind free of kamma and free of the kammic manifestation of rebirth.

Once kamma ceases there will be no more births. Without kamma to create the unfolding need for continued existence, rebirth ends.

The Buddha's understanding and teaching on rebirth differ greatly from the Brahmanism of the Buddha's time and differs greatly with many of the mystical Buddhist religions. The Dhamma also differs greatly from the Hindu and Hindu-influenced beliefs that would arise well after the Buddha's passing.

Many religions, including some Buddhist religions, teach morals and ethics as a way of hopefully having ever more pleasurable future lives, but never abandoning conditioned thinking and continued I-making. This is continued clinging to an idea of an ego-self and is specifically what the Buddha was referring to when he said:

"This was the third knowledge I attained in the third watch of the night. Ignorance was destroyed; knowledge arose; darkness was destroyed; light arose — as happens in one who is heedful, ardent, & resolute. Birth is ended, the holy life fulfilled, the task done. There is nothing further for this world." [62]

Reincarnation is the belief that an individual and permanent soul travels throughout time as the same spiritual entity appearing in a different physical body life after life. This cannot be reconciled with the teachings of not-self, emptiness, dependent origination, the five clinging-aggregates and kamma. The self that would reincarnate has been shown to be an impermanent aggregate of physical and mental factors sustained only in the present instant by craving and clinging.

The Buddha in describing Dukkha or suffering teaches: "Birth is suffering, sickness is suffering, old age is suffering." The Four Noble Truths directly teach the cessation of suffering and the cessation of birth, death and rebirth. The Buddha did not teach a

we're feeding ith- which can only produce stress + suffering

unfettered = uninhibited, uncontrolled

way of manipulating a more pleasurable future birth, he taught a way of leaving the recurring cycle of dukkha behind.

This brings up the notion of annihilation. Annihilation is an extreme view rooted in the ignorance of anatta. It is an ego-personality's fear of annihilation that creates this doubt and reaction as the ego-personality is always vigilant about continuation. This creates a need of establishing the ego-self in the future.

A skillful way of considering kamma and rebirth is to view kamma driving the birth of this present moment. It is past actions that have brought you here. In order to complete the path, to end craving and clinging and to bring dukkha to cessation, giving birth to another moment of clinging to objects, views, and ideas is unskillful.

What is most skillful is to recognize the causes of continued confusion and suffering and to abandon those causes. The next moment holds the potential to be free of confusion and suffering. The next moment holds the potential for freedom from continued rebirth of anatta.

When you abandon craving and clinging your immediate future is free of confusion and suffering.

The distracting questions rooted in ignorant views no longer arise. You are no longer experiencing the results of past kamma and there is no longer any ongoing "birth" of confusion and suffering.

This is the most skillful way to consider birth, death, and rebirth. This moment holds the potential for the next moment. Ignorance will bring more confusion and unsatisfactoriness. Refined mindfulness and deep concentration, developed within the framework of the Eightfold Path, brings profound wisdom and understanding of The Four Noble Truths. From wisdom in this moment brings a life free of ignorance, confusion, and stress.

It is a common reaction from an ego-personality insisting on continued establishment of "self" to continue to cling to form and resist or ignore the truth of ending rebirth. As anatta must establish itself in every object, event, view, or idea, the ego-self cannot accept any future thought or idea that does not include the ego-self. An awakened mind, free of craving and clinging, peacefully experiences life as life occurs with no limiting and stress-inducing self-referential thoughts or actions.

As stated, the Five Clinging-Aggregates are the vehicle for the "self" that experiences dukkha. This ego-self, or conditioned mind, is impermanent, or "empty" of any permanent and individually originated constituents. There is no "self" and no kamma other than the conditioned mind manifested due to specific causes and conditions arising in the phenomenal world.

The Buddha never taught emptiness as a mystical realm that somehow is both empty but includes the phenomenal world. As with all of the Dhamma, emptiness was used in relation to suffering and The Four Noble Truths. He taught that one should "empty oneself of clinging" and that The Five Clinging-Aggregates are "empty" of any permanence or substance. He taught that one should "empty" the world of self, to cease "I-making."

"'Kamma should be known. The cause by which kamma comes into play should be known. The diversity in kamma should be known. The result of kamma should be known. The cessation of kamma should be known. The path of practice leading to the cessation of kamma should be known.' Thus it has been said. Why was it said?

"Intention, I tell you, is kamma. Intending, one does kamma by way of body, speech, & intellect.

"And what is the result of kamma? The result of kamma is of three sorts, I tell you: that which arises right here & now, that which arises later [in this lifetime], and that which arises following that.

"And what is the cessation of kamma? From the cessation of contact is the cessation of kamma; and just this noble eightfold path — right view, right resolve, right speech, right action, right livelihood, right effort, right mindfulness, right concentration — is the path of practice leading to the cessation of kamma.

"Now when a noble disciple discerns kamma in this way, the cause by which kamma comes into play in this way, the diversity of kamma in this way, the result of kamma in this way, the cessation of kamma in this way, & the path of practice leading to the cessation of kamma in this way, then he discerns this penetrative integrated life as the cessation of kamma. With the cessation of kamma comes the cessation of rebirth of The Five Clinging-Aggregates."
63

This Week's Dhamma Study

- Listen to the week nine talk on Kamma and Rebirth: http://crossrivermeditation.com/truth-of-happiness-online-course-talks/

- Continue with your meditation practice in the morning and early evening. If you feel comfortable with adding a few minutes to your practice do so. Ten to Twenty minute meditation sessions should be comfortable for you.

- In meditation, remain mindful of your breathing as you dispassionately notice feelings and thoughts arise and dissipate. When you notice that you are caught up in your own thoughts and have lost awareness of your breath, put aside the focus on your thoughts and place your awareness on your breathing. Become aware of your mind from a dispassionate observational view, a mind-state of choiceless awareness always mindful of your breath.

- At the end of your meditation sessions take a moment to notice the quality of your mind. Be at peace with the quality of your mind.

- Continue to develop wisdom by noticing your attachments to the people and events of your life, including yourself. Continue to generate the Right Intention to let go of all attachments and all impermanent views.

- In your day-to-day life notice when you are engaged in Right Speech, Action and Livelihood and when you are not. Develop the strong intention to abandon all wrong speech, action and livelihood. As concentration deepens, non-virtuous thoughts, words and deeds become apparent.

- Continue to develop Right Effort. Put aside time for a regular meditation practice and maintain a priority to your practice. There will always be life events distracting away from practice. Very rarely will these events be more immediate or important than putting aside some time twice a day for a period of meditation. Bring mindfulness into all areas of your life by staying focused in the present moment.

- Notice any persistent thoughts and your awareness of the impermanence of all thoughts. Avoid being analytical. This is a dispassionate observance of thoughts and feelings as they arise and pass away. Take note of developing a more mindful presence in your life. Notice when you are fully present with another. Notice when you are not as distracted or reactive.

- Continue your Dhamma study with week ten.

- Always be gentle with yourself and enjoy your practice!

If taking the correspondence course:

- Write a paragraph or two regarding your Dhamma practice and write down any questions or insights into impermanence and how impermanence contributes to stress. Note your deepening understanding of how impermanence and clinging give rise to the stress and unhappiness of the ego-personality.

- Write an additional paragraph or two regarding your understanding of the cause of kamma and rebirth and the ending of kamma and rebirth.

- To submit your writing, please use this form: http://crossrivermeditation.com/home-study-submissions/

- I will respond to you within 24 to 48 hours.

Week Ten

Hindrances to Maintaining
a Dhamma Practice

At Savatthi the Buddha addressed those assembled:

"Friends, there are five obstacles to be overcome, five hindrances that weaken and distract from the Eightfold Path. These five are:

- Sensual Desire

- Ill Will

- Laziness and Drowsiness

- Restlessness and Anxiety

- Uncertainty, Skepticism and Doubt

"These obstacles can overwhelm your mindfulness and confuse wise discernment. When a dhamma practitioner has not yet abandoned these five hindrances it will be impossible for them to understand what is for their benefit or for the benefit of others. It will be impossible to become an awakened human being settled in equanimity, settled in direct knowledge and clear vision.

"Just as a swift-flowing river carrying everything with it, if diverted by side-channels on both sides, the current in the middle of the river would become dispersed, diffused, dissipated. It could no longer travel far and clearly.

"In the same way, when a practitioner has not abandoned these five obstacles, hindrances that overwhelm mindfulness and confuse discernment, they will no longer understand what is for their own benefit or others. Not knowing what is skillful they will not develop understanding or release. Equanimity, direct knowledge, and clear vision will not develop.

"Now, when a dhamma practitioner has abandoned these five obstacles, these hindrances, they will develop refined and useful mindfulness and clear discernment. Wise, they will understand what is for their benefit and for other's benefit. They will develop equanimity, direct knowledge and clear vision. Released, they are free from confusion, delusion, and stress. They are unbound.

"In the same way as the practitioner free of hindrances, the river, with the side-channels closed would run swift and clear to its destination with nothing to diffuse, disperse, or dissipate it.

"In the same manner, free of obstacles, free of hindrances, the wise ones reach their goal.

"Suppose there were a river, flowing down from the mountains — going far, its current swift, carrying everything with it — and a person would close the channels leading away from it on both sides, so that the current in the middle of the river would be un-dispersed, un-diffused, & un-dissipated; it would go far, its current swift, carrying everything with it.

"In the same way, when a practitioner has abandoned these five obstacles, hindrances that overwhelm awareness and weaken discernment, when they are strong in discernment they will easily understand what is for their own benefit and for the benefit of others. They will develop equanimity, direct knowledge and clear vision. Released, they are free from confusion, delusion, and stress. They are unbound." [64]

The first hindrance to establishing a meditation practice is distraction from sensual desire. Distracted by things that appeal to your senses prevents you from being mindful of practice. Often your mind will want to remain distracted by the many activities of your day. You tell yourself that you are too busy to meditate.

Your mind, at first, may want to avoid meditation. When you meditate despite this common tendency, you will diminish this tendency and you begin to gain control of your mind and your life.

In meditation you may be distracted by an infinite number of craving thoughts. Whatever craving thoughts arise, recognize desire as a distraction. Remain mindful of the thought or thoughts, recognizing that they are a hindrance to practice. These thoughts are as impermanent as any other thought.

Dispassionately let thoughts go and return your mindfulness to your breathing. This is the basic practice and continued practice will diminish sensory desire and return your mind to its natural calm and well-concentrated state.

Ill will, or holding harsh judgments, anger and resentments toward others, or yourself, can make it almost impossible to continue with meditation practice. Recognize that the cause of the ill will is your own desire that the people and events of your life be different than they are, or that you perceive them to be.

If persistent thoughts of ill will arise, dispassionately stay with the thoughts for a moment or two, and return your mindfulness to the sensation of breathing.

As your awareness of the origins of ill will increases, maintain a mind of equanimity. As best as you can, remain free of judgment of the people and events of your life. This takes Right Effort and consistent practice, and with time you can free yourself of the hindrance of ill will.

Practicing Metta meditation, is a skillful aid in releasing harsh judgments. Practice metta whenever harsh judgments of yourself or others is making it difficult to quiet your mind. Once your mind has quieted using metta, resume shamatha-vipassana meditation.

Sloth, torpor, drowsiness or laziness affect everyone at one time or another. It is most skillful to recognize this as aversion to practice. It is your conditioned mind's way of avoiding the freedom that will arise from consistent dhamma practice.

Drowsiness is often nothing more than a manifestation of resistance to meditation and dhamma practice. Meditating despite occasional drowsiness will interrupt this reaction.

If drowsiness or sleepiness is a true physical problem arising from a lack of sleep or too much activity, it is appropriate to rest for awhile and then resume meditation. Check your posture. Lying down or not sitting up straight can contribute to drowsiness.

Drowsiness is another hindrance to practice that is to be dealt with through equanimity and persistence. Recognize that it is affecting you and your practice and stay with your practice. Drowsiness will fall away.

Restlessness is an aspect of boredom. Boredom is your conditioned mind's need for constant stimulation and distraction. Restlessness and worry can be difficult hindrances to overcome. Persistence will show results. If restlessness and worry have risen to the level of anxiety, it may be best to meditate for shorter periods of time and more often.

Remind yourself that just for the meditation period you will be putting aside restlessness and anxiety and maintain your awareness on your breath. Meditation has proven to be a very effective way of putting anxiety causing thoughts aside and staying mindful of life as life occurs.

Doubt, uncertainty and skepticism can be hindrances at any stage of Dhamma practice. Great doubt can deepen one's practice if the doubt is allowed to be a part of practice, letting doubt be doubt and mindfully continuing with practice.

Other people's skepticism can be a hindrance as well, especially people that do not understand the Dhamma or the purpose of meditation practice. The most effective way to work through uncertainty, doubt and skepticism is to engage in practice wholeheartedly without any unrealistic expectations.

Examine your motivations for practice. Is your intention for engaging in meditation practice to put aside craving and desire born of ignorance (of The Four Noble Truths) or is it to "fix" an ego-self? Attempting to fix or satisfy an ego-self only continues confusion and stress. Uncertainty and skepticism will arise if your view or intention is to fix a broken or flawed self. You meditate to mindfully develop concentration and develop mindfulness of all clinging, craving, aversion and desire.

Hindrances or distractions will arise. They will have no permanent effect on your practice if you persevere. Hindrances are recognized mind states to be aware of. Be with them as dispassionately as possible. As long as you continue with your practice, hindrances will arise and subside until they no longer are a part of your conditioned thinking.

By putting aside resistance to meditation practice you will strengthen your resolve and begin to diminish your mind's natural tendency to resist the quiet and spacious mind developed by a true and effective meditation practice.

Always avoid judging yourself or your practice harshly. Do the best you can and be gentle with yourself. Maintain a consistent Shamatha-Vipassana meditation practice within the framework of The Eightfold Path and you will develop lasting peace and happiness.

The second and sixth factors of The Eightfold Path, Right Intention and Right Effort, greatly support your overall Dhamma practice. Maintaining the strong resolve of Right Intention and engaging in Right Effort will provide the framework needed to develop and maintain a Dhamma practice. Right Intention is holding in mind the intention to put aside clinging, aversion and delusional thinking and awaken.

Being mindful of Right Intention and Right Effort, you make a commitment to meditation practice and developing your understanding of the Eightfold Path. Put aside set times, preferably twice a day and approximately 12 hours apart, if possible, for meditation practice. It is most effective to meditate as soon as possible after waking before becoming distracted or sidetracked by your daily routine. A second session approximately 12 hours later provides balance and deepens mindfulness and concentration. Doing this consistently begins to diminish your conditioned mind's need for distraction.

Right Effort (the sixth factor of The Eightfold Path) is keeping yourself in fit physical, mental and spiritual condition as well. Getting enough rest, eating healthy, and physical exercise are all a part of Right Effort. Any exercise is a support for Dhamma practice and walking "meditation" is a very skillful way to combine exercise and mindful movement. Tai Chi and QiGong are particularly supportive of Dhamma practice. Keep in mind that there is no effective substitute for sitting meditation. Bringing the body to stillness greatly supports a calm and tranquil mind.

Many wholesome practices can be beneficial to one's health and well-being and yoga can also be helpful to Dhamma practice. It should be noted that the underlying Hindu philosophies are sometimes contradictory to the Buddha's direct teachings. If practicing yoga, or other disciplines, it is skillful to resist the modern view of merging different practices into one "unified" practice. Subtle but vitally important aspects are often diminished, or abandoned completely, when attempting to create a "unified dhamma."

One last thing: Joining a like-minded community of Dhamma practitioners greatly supports an individual practice. Joining a community of Dhamma practitioners will provide a weekly structure to your practice. A qualified teacher will notice if you are losing direction or focus, and the community as a whole will support you with their own insights and you will be able to support your sangha.

This Week's Dhamma Study

- Listen to the week ten talk on Hindrances to Practice:

  http://crossrivermeditation.com/truth-of-happiness-online-course-talks/

- Continue with your meditation practice in the morning and early evening. If you feel comfortable with adding a few minutes to your practice do so. Ten to Twenty minute meditation sessions should be comfortable for you.

- In meditation, remain mindful of your breathing as you dispassionately notice feelings and thoughts arise and dissipate. When you notice that you are caught up in your own thoughts and have lost awareness of your breath, put aside the focus on your thoughts and place your awareness on your breathing. Become aware of your mind from a dispassionate observational view, a mind-state of choiceless awareness always mindful of your breath.

• At the end of your meditation sessions take a moment to notice the quality of your mind. Be at peace with the quality of your mind.

• Continue to develop wisdom by noticing your attachments to the people and events of your life, including yourself. Continue to generate the Right Intention to let go of all attachments and all impermanent views.

• In your day-to-day life notice when you are engaged in Right Speech, Action and Livelihood and when you are not. Develop the strong intention to abandon all wrong speech, action and livelihood. As concentration deepens, non-virtuous thoughts, words and deeds become apparent.

• Continue to develop Right Effort. Put aside time for a regular meditation practice and maintain a priority to your practice. There will always be life events distracting away from practice. Very rarely will these events be more immediate or important than putting aside some time twice a day for a period of meditation. Bring mindfulness into all areas of your life by staying focused in the present moment.

- Be mindful of any persistent thoughts and your awareness of the impermanence of all thoughts. Avoid being analytical. This is a dispassionate observance of thoughts and feelings as they arise and pass away. Be mindful of developing a more mindful presence in your life. Notice when you are fully present with another. Notice when you are not as distracted or reactive.

- Please read my closing words in the next chapter.

- **Congratulations on completing your ten-week Dhamma Study. Please continue to be gentle with yourself, enjoy your practice and deepening understanding of developing lasting peace and happiness! Please stay in touch!**

If taking the correspondence course:

- Write a short paragraph regarding your meditation practice and write down any questions or insights into impermanence and how impermanence contributes to stress and unhappiness. Note your deepening understanding of how impermanence and clinging give rise to the stress and unhappiness of the ego-personality.

- Write an additional paragraph or two regarding any hindrances to your practice that you notice and how you react or respond to them.

- To submit your writing, please use this form: http://crossrivermeditation.com/home-study-submissions/

- Send me an email to schedule a phone or online video chat instruction session. Please request a few half-hour time periods on Thursdays between 10 am and 8:30 pm, Fridays between 10 am and 8:30 pm, Saturdays between 11 am and 2:30 pm or Sundays between 10 am and 1 pm. These are Eastern Times. John@CrossRiverMeditation.com

- I will respond to you within 24 to 48 hours.

- Please read my closing words in the next chapter.

- **Congratulations on completing your ten-week Dhamma Study. Please continue to be gentle with yourself, enjoy your practice and deepening understanding of developing lasting peace and happiness! Please stay in touch!**

Closing Instruction

You have now completed ten weeks of well-focused Dhamma instruction. You may already be noticing a more present and peaceful mindfulness in your day-to-day life. This is not to be taken lightly. Recognizing the practical benefits of these profound teachings is an important part of developing heightened mindfulness of the entire Dhamma.

The Buddha often told those he was teaching "Ehipassiko" meaning "come and see for yourself." These teachings do not take us to other-worldly realms that have no practical benefit. The distraction of unsatisfactoriness, unhappiness, and stress occur in this phenomenal world.

With present-moment-mindfulness of the Dhamma you will deepen your awareness of the distraction of dukkha. Awareness is not change itself but it is what brings the power to change. Be very gentle with yourself and avoid harsh judgments of yourself or your practice. Be mindful of the entire Eightfold Path and how each factor supports and informs your deepening wisdom, virtue and concentration.

Engage in your Dhamma practice whole-heartedly and with patient forbearance. If you have a local sangha that is well-focused on The Four Noble Truths become a part of the sangha. If there is not a well-focused sangha in your area consider starting one. If you want to use this course as part of a ten-week course for your sangha, please let me know and I will help as I can.

Dhamma practice does take time and Right Effort to develop. The true lineage of the Dhamma began over 2,500 years ago. At the Buddha's first teaching he set the wheel of truth in motion. As The Four Noble Truths have entered each mind ready to receive these profound truths the lineage of the three jewels has been maintained. This is a true Dhamma lineage and a true Dhamma transmission.

Beginning with the awakened mind of one human being, Shakyamuni Gautama, The Buddha, the lineage of the Dhamma is now a part of your mind. Treat it like the precious jewel that it is and lasting peace and happiness will arise in your mind as well.

The following chapter on The Precepts and The Paramitas will be a support to your developing Dhamma practice.

The Precepts and The Paramitas

The Precepts

Jiddu Krishnamurti often said "Look at the lives you are living." He was stressing the importance of being mindfully present in thought, word and deed in our interaction with others and with ourselves.

As a way of integrating The Four Noble Truths into our daily lives, and as a simple and effective way of being mindful of how we relate to the phenomenal world, the Buddha gave us precepts. Precepts are simply principles for conduct. By following these precepts in thought, word and deed we are living within the framework of The Eightfold Path.

The Buddha taught five basic lay precepts and then three additional principles for those considering monastic life, and sometimes for those on retreat. The Buddha also taught, depending on the source and the subsequent Buddhist sect or school, 200 or more precepts for monastics. Most of the additional monastic precepts are for conduct within a spiritual community or monastery.

The five Buddhist Precepts for lay people are:

1. Refrain from killing or taking life. Act with good-will and loving-kindness.
2. Refrain from stealing or taking what is not freely given. Be generous.
3. Refrain from false, unnecessary, misleading, harmful or impatient speech. Speak with kindness, honesty and mindfulness.
4. Refrain from sexual misconduct or using sex in a selfish or harmful manner. Be content and giving.
5. Refrain form the use of intoxicants so to be mindful and thoughtful.

The Eightfold Path is a path of virtue, concentration and wisdom, and by being mindful of behavior in relation to these simple precepts, you will develop more virtuous lives. This will deepen your meditation practice, developing deeper concentration. As you become more mindful of virtue and concentration, wisdom deepens.

Wisdom is further developed and expressed by living life with the gentleness that comes from following these precepts.

On the surface these precepts are fairly easy to abide by. As you look deeper at your intentions and intentional actions you may become aware of subtle aspects of clinging, craving, desire and aversion keeping you stuck in conditioned thinking. Do you hold a persistent view of yourself or others that is not in keeping with these precepts?

Do you engage in character assassination, including what you are saying to yourself? Are your thoughts free from aggressive and hurtful thoughts towards others and yourself? Do you try to "kill" another's spirit through hurtful comments, or imposing negative views of self? Do you gossip or tell small lies? Do you treat sex as a mindful expression of generosity or simply a means of satiating your own desires? Do you take (even emotionally) what is not freely given? Do you obsessively or addictively use drugs, alcohol, TV, food, yoga, golf, work or anything else to escape the reality of your life?

Obsessive behavior of any kind is an expression of discursive conditioned thinking caused by the manifestations of craving and clinging.

While the initial guidance gained from The Precepts is very important, careful consideration of each precept will reveal a much deeper and broader application, and the application of The Precepts will differ for each everyone. For example, we all agree that the intentional taking of another human beings life is wrong. Is killing still wrong in the context of war? What about the killing of animals as a food source? Is it wrong to step on a bug or pluck a tick off of a pet? These questions need to be answered in accordance with each individual's own mindful conscience, and will more than likely change over time and as Dhamma practice develops.

It is quite obvious that these precepts describe an enlightened way of living. The Precepts as an aid, and truthfully a necessity, to Dhamma practice may not be immediately apparent. The awareness gained by Dhamma practice will enhance your awareness of the precepts and a more skillful way of living. Living mindfully with the precepts will greatly enhance overall Dhamma practice.

When you bring yourself to your cushion to sit, you bring all of you. It is much more difficult to realize your true, unfettered self when you are bothered by thoughts of un-skillful actions. The more you can adhere to the guidelines of The Precepts, the more peaceful your life will be, the more loving your relationships will be, and the closer you will be to expressing your true mindful nature.

From an entirely liberated view the precepts lead to being mindful of how you can enhance the life experience of others and free yourself from discursive conditioned behavior. You learn how to use your speech in a loving and compassionate way to bring healing and liberation to yourself and others. Your sexual relations are characterized by gentleness and giving. You develop great generosity of spirit. You keep your body pure and your mind clear resulting in well-concentrated virtuous acts arising from wisdom.

Meditation practice develops concentration and insight of conditioned thinking. Holding in mind, being mindful of The Eightfold Path and the Precepts you are able to remain mindful of conditioned thinking and how conditioned thinking arises in your daily life. As less-than-skillful thoughts, words and deeds arise while maintaining mindfulness of the precepts in this present moment, you are able to clearly see the results of clinging, craving and desire. With this insight you are now able to put these distracting and discursive mind states aside with complete mindfulness of their cause and resulting condition.

Your very life, moment by moment, becomes Dhamma practice. You stay present with whatever mind state arises, without aversion, gaining deeper and deeper insight into your own mind. Ultimately, through a complete practice of integrating The Eightfold Path into your life and being mindful of these precepts, you are able to recognize all conditioned thinking.

An effective way of incorporating these precepts into your life is to spend a few minutes during your sitting practice to review mindfully how you have practiced these principles in your daily life. When you start your day you can develop the strong intention to keep the precepts and to be mindful of them.

Being mindful of these basic precepts in your life will greatly increase your awareness of less than skillful thoughts and actions. Being mindful of your present moment's thoughts, words and deeds is key to deepening insight into your mind and putting aside conditioned thinking.

Unpleasant or agitated mind states that arise, whether fleeting or persistent, are all born of desire. Desire is a reaction due to ignorance of The Four Noble Truths. Out of a perceived need to be different than you are in this present moment, a choice is made that more of what brings pleasure should be pursued and what brings unpleasantness should be avoided.

Avoidance or aversion is also pursuit through worry, self-doubt, harsh judgments and fear. Aversion is the desire that a past or present experience be different than experienced, or a desire that a future event be different than expected.

Holding in mind negative mind states is mindfulness arising from conditioned thinking. This unskillful mindful pursuit leads to more craving and aversion and more delusional thinking. Often being mindful of negative mind states is viewed as a way of understanding how these mind states were caused.

A singular phenomenal cause is impossible to determine. Attempting to isolate a specific singular cause will only lead to more discursive thinking. All stress arises from manifestations of desire, and once acknowledged within the context of The Eightfold Path and the Precepts, insight arises and the reaction of conditioned mind is interrupted.

By following these five precepts, you will develop a moral and ethical life, liberated and free from harmful actions and reactions. You will be able to develop deeper levels of skillful mindfulness.

Through mindfulness of The Four Noble Truths including The Eightfold Path, and by holding in mind the Precepts, you are placing mindful awareness on the path of liberation and freedom and ceasing mindfulness of stress-causing desire.

A complete Dhamma practice of mindfully integrating The Four Noble Truths will lead to liberation and freedom from stress, confusion and suffering. Holding in mind the precepts in thought, word and deed develops a gentle and compassionate integrity to practice.

The Paramitas

The word "Paramita" means "Great Perfections." These are qualities of mind to, at first, generate through Dhamma practice and then to be mindful of them as a way of remaining focused on the Dhamma. Incorporating through Right Intention to hold to these perfections of thought, word, and deed develops focus and patience. The Paramitas also provide a framework for viewing progress along the way.

Sariputta, one of the Buddha's chief disciples, questioned the Buddha one day: "How many qualities are there to be developed in the Dhamma?"

The Buddha responded: "There are ten qualities developed in the Dhamma. What are the ten? Giving, virtue, renunciation, wisdom, energy, patience, truthfulness, determination, loving-kindness, and equanimity are qualities developed in the Dhamma." [65]

Giving, or Dana, is the first perfection and incorporates all of the other perfections. In fact, there is an aspect of each paramita in all the other paramitas. These are qualities we all possess and are developed further as the behaviors rooted in greed, aversion and delusion are put aside

The ten Paramitas can be integrated into Dhamma practice by bringing each paramita to mind directly after shamatha-vipassana meditation and generating the intention to remain mindful of each paramita. This will incline the mind towards thoughts that are in keeping the qualities of these Great Perfections moment to moment.

These ten perfections of behavior are all aspects of The Eightfold Path and when developed free the mind from greed, aversion and further deluded thinking. When fully developed, the mind remains at peace and unmoved from impermanence of phenomenal life.

Holding in mind and acting in accordance with these ten perfections directly influences the unfolding of kamma. Our present moment intentional acts determine the unfolding of our past intentional acts.

Being mindful of these ten paramitas will support the development of lasting peace and happiness.

The Ratana Sutta

The Three Jewels

The Three Refuges

Nearly all schools of Buddhism refer to "The Three Jewels" and taking refuge in them. The Three Jewels are also called "The Three Refuges." Refuge is a place or state of mind that is a protection or a shelter from hardship or danger. Refuge is a place or state of mind that is a source of comfort and peace.

The Three Jewels are:

1. The Buddha
2. The Dhamma
3. The Sangha

In Buddhism when one takes refuge one is taking refuge in these precious jewels. The ritual of taking refuge is a formal, and usually public, statement of holding the strong intention to have the example of the Buddha and the teachings of the Dhamma be the framework for awakening, along with supporting and receiving the support of a community of Dhamma practitioners, the Sangha.

The teaching known as the "Jewel Discourse" or the "Ratana Sutta" was given in the city of Vesali at a time of widespread famine and spreading disease. There were many dead bodies as the conditions overwhelmed the ability of the townspeople to properly dispose of bodies. The local citizens sought out the Buddha's help, who was nearby in Rajagaha.

The Buddha arrived in Vesali a short time later with a large number of monks, including Ananda. Just before the Buddha's arrival torrential rains helped the situation somewhat by cleansing the landscape of rotting corpses and clearing the air and water.

The Buddha presented this teaching to an entire city overcome by physical and emotional suffering.

Prior to his presenting this discourse he instructed his attending monks to walk through the city and do what they could to ease the physical suffering of the citizens and to individually present this teaching. At the formal teaching the Buddha then presented a way to bring true refuge from the stress and suffering of the world and to put an end to all dukkha:

"May all beings assembled have peace of mind. May all beings assembled listen mindfully to these words. May you all radiate goodwill and loving-kindness to all who offer help and understanding to you. Understand this: "There is no more precious jewel, no more refuge, no more comfort, than the Buddha. As woodland groves in the early heat of summer are crowned with blossoming flowers, so is the sublime Dhamma leading to the calm and peace of nibbana. The peerless and excellent awakened one, the teacher of true understanding, the teacher of the Noble Path is the Buddha, The one who has awakened."

Here the Buddha is not teaching worship of himself. The Buddha often referred to himself as the "Tathagata," the one who has gone forth. The Buddha had gone forth from distraction and ignorance, stress and suffering, to well-concentrated wisdom, liberation and freedom. Through his own efforts the Buddha awakened. The Buddha is here offering himself as the example of one human being going forth on The Eightfold Path and awakening.

Taking refuge in the Buddha is understanding that all human beings can go forth from ignorance and attain wisdom and Right Understanding. There is great inspiration and comfort in understanding that liberation and freedom is possible for all human beings.

The Buddha continues: "There is no more precious jewel than the teachings of the Buddha, the Dhamma. Understanding this brings true liberation and freedom. The Buddha, calm and mindful has experienced the cessation of clinging and desire. The Deathless state of nibbana has been attained. The Buddha teaches the Noble Eightfold Path that unfailingly brings concentration, liberation and freedom. There is no more precious jewel than the Dhamma."

The Buddha is describing that there is a precious jewel in taking refuge in the path of liberation and freedom. In this setting in Vesali, the Buddha is teaching that once practical needs have been taken care of to turn one's attention to being mindful of the teachings of the Buddha.

The Buddha continues: "There is no more precious jewel than the Sangha. Understanding this brings true liberation and freedom. The virtuous ones who bring the Dhamma, they are the Jewel of The Sangha. Those with steadfast minds, free of clinging, they are the jewel of the Sangha. Those that understand with wisdom The Four Noble Truths, they are the jewel of the Sangha. Those that gain true insight and abandon self-delusion, doubt, and indulgence in meaningless rites and rituals, They are the jewel of the sangha. Those beyond despair and evil-doings, They are the jewel of the sangha. Those whose understanding arises from the support of the sangha, who can no longer conceal the truth from themselves due to the sangha, they are the precious jewel of the sangha. Those whose kamma is extinguished, the future of no concern, with rebirth ending, due to the support of the sangha, this is the precious jewel of the sangha." [66]

The example of the Buddha's life, the teachings of the Buddha, the Dhamma, and the Sangha, provide refuge from the unsatisfactoriness, confusion, and suffering inherent in the world. Being mindful of the three jewels concentrates the mind to what is of utmost importance.

Taking Refuge in the Three Jewels is taking great comfort in understanding that awakening is possible for any human being. The example of the Buddha's life shows that.

There is great comfort in realizing that The Eightfold Path is a path accessible and easily integrated by anyone.

There is also great comfort in knowing that we do not engage in the path of liberation and freedom alone. The Buddha often said that the most important aspect of practice is the sangha. The support and commitment that we gain from each other often provides the encouragement and strength to continue, even when difficult times interfere.

Holding in mind the Three Jewels provides continual direction for one's mindfulness.

Taking refuge in the Buddha, The Dhamma and the Sangha also provides a framework for mindful expression of joy and freedom.

The Fire Discourse

The Buddha presented his first two discourses to the ascetics he had previously befriended. The first discourse on The Four Noble Truths explained the cause of delusion in the world and the path to understanding. The second discourse explained how the perception of individuality arises and what forms the belief in "self."

About one month after the Buddha's first two discourses, he presented The Fire Discourse to approximately 1,000 followers. Upon hearing this short discourse, most of those in attendance awakened.

At that time in northern India and Nepal there were various cults who engaged in ritualistic worship, sacrifice, and mystical practices. One of these cults was a popular fire cult, devoted to rituals using fire. The Buddha used the fire-worshippers as an analogy to how individual personalities "worship" what contacts the senses.

The Fire Discourse presented below is a brief but insightful look at how the physical senses interpreted by the intellect reinforce the belief in "self."

The Buddha was staying in Gaya, at Gaya Head, with 1,000 monks. There he addressed the monks:

"Monks, the All is aflame. What All is aflame? The eye is aflame. Forms are aflame. Consciousness at the eye is aflame. Contact at the eye is aflame. And whatever there is that arises in dependence on contact at the eye - experienced as pleasure, pain or neither-pleasure-nor-pain - that too is aflame. Aflame with what? Aflame with the fire of passion, the fire of aversion, the fire of delusion. Aflame, I tell you, with birth, aging & death, with sorrows, lamentations, pains, distresses, & despairs.

The ear is aflame. Sounds are aflame...

The nose is aflame. Aromas are aflame...

The tongue is aflame...

Flavors are aflame...

The body is aflame...

Tactile sensations are aflame...

The intellect is aflame...

Ideas are aflame...

Consciousness at the intellect is aflame...

Contact at the intellect is aflame...

And whatever there is that arises in dependence on contact at the intellect - experienced as pleasure, pain or neither-pleasure-nor-pain - that too is aflame. "

"Aflame with what? Aflame with the fire of passion, the fire of aversion, the fire of delusion. Aflame, I say, with birth, aging & death, with sorrows, lamentations, pains, distresses, & despairs.

"Seeing thus, the well-instructed disciple of the noble ones grows disenchanted with the eye, disenchanted with forms, disenchanted with consciousness at the eye, disenchanted with contact at the eye. And whatever there is that arises in dependence on contact at the eye, experienced as pleasure, pain or neither-pleasure-nor-pain: With that, too, he grows disenchanted.

He grows disenchanted with the ear...

He grows disenchanted with the nose...

He grows disenchanted with the tongue...

He grows disenchanted with the body...

He grows disenchanted with the intellect, disenchanted with ideas, disenchanted with consciousness at the intellect, disenchanted with contact at the intellect.

And whatever there is that arises in dependence on contact at the intellect, experienced as pleasure, pain or neither-pleasure-nor-pain: He grows disenchanted with that too. Disenchanted, he becomes dispassionate. Through dispassion, he is fully released. With full release, there is the knowledge, 'Fully released.' He discerns that 'Birth is ended, the holy life fulfilled, the task done. There is nothing further for this world.'"

That is what the Blessed One said. Gratified, the monks delighted at his words. And while this explanation was being given, the hearts of the 1,000 monks, through no clinging (not being sustained), were fully released from fermentation and effluents. 67

The Buddha is teaching that through Dependent Origination the components that make up the self are "inflamed" by the passions that arise from desire and aversion. This passion drives the worship (attachment) of sensory fulfillment and reinforces dukkha (suffering).

It is the preoccupation with dukkha that perpetuates delusion. The lesson to the 1,000 followers was how delusion and a wrong view of self arises and is maintained. The Buddha taught that reacting to phenomenon contacting the senses creates an identity that is attached to those sensations.

The Eightfold Path is the framework for mindful recognition of the origination of dukkha and for abandoning its causes.

Awakening occurs as understanding develops through The Eightfold Path. Through The Eightfold Path understanding of the nature of reality arises and disenchantment with the six senses develops. Disenchanted with constant sensory fulfillment, the mind quiets and wisdom arises.

The development of an ego-self through the Five Clinging-Aggregates is maintained by discursive thinking fueled by desire. Developing Right View or Right Understanding brings renunciation. The strong attachment to the wrong view of self manifests as hindrances to practice.

Doubt rooted in an identity of self and the constant need for sensory input are to be recognized and abandoned. Doubt rooted in an identity of self manifests as an unwillingness to accept anything that would diminish or negate the image of self.

A defining characteristic of a mind stuck in wrong view is restlessness, always seeking sensory stimulation. The Eightfold Path, including Shamatha-Vipassana meditation, is the path of direct experience that ends doubt and brings insight to sense experience.

The Eightfold Path develops a tranquil mind with the ability to see passions as they arise. With a tranquil mind, insight, and Right Intention, the mind is free to develop lasting peace and happiness.

Final Words

Thank You for taking this Dhamma course and allowing me to be your "teacher" for these ten weeks. I am honored to have done so. My skillful wish is that you have found this Dhamma study helpful in developing understanding of The Four Noble Truths and the Buddha's Eightfold Path for developing lasting peace and happiness.

If you have found this book and course helpful, please consider writing a review and posting it at Amazon.com. Thank You.

For more Dhamma articles, recorded Dhamma talks, class and retreat schedule, please visit CrossRiverMeditation.com.

Twitter: @johnh_crmc

Google+: google.com/+CrossRiverMeditation

Author's Biography

John's first steps on the path of liberation and freedom began in earnest in 1981 when he first learned Transcendental Meditation (a mantra or object based technique) from a wonderful teacher, Maggie Schluyter, who patiently and lovingly guided John through his early practice.

Over time John encountered many wonderful teachers and spiritual disciplines. John has always been drawn to Eastern philosophies in general and the teachings of the Buddha in particular.

Having studied in many of the different schools of Buddhism, in May 2010, John took his Vows of Refuge and The Vow of the Boddhisattva at the Kamma Triyana Dharmachakra Monastery from his teacher at the time Khenpo Karthur, Rinpoche. Rinpoche bestowed on John the names "Karma Tingzin Gyurme" (Unchangeable Meditation) during the Taking Of Refuge Ceremony, and "Jampa Tarchin" (Perfection of Love) during the Boddhisattva Ceremony.

Names are given during these sacred ceremonies not necessarily so that the recipient will change their name, (although we are all free to do so) but as a reminder and definition of one's purpose now that vows have been taken. John's intention is to continue to follow the essential nature of his vows.

John has always found a measure of truth and understanding in many of the different Buddhist schools, and other spiritual disciplines. John studied and practiced the teachings of Zen Buddhism as taught by the early patriarchs, Boddhidharma, Hui-Neng, Huang-Po, and today by Master Sheng Yen, John Daido Loori, DT Suzuki, Shunryu Suzuki, Kosho Uchiyama, and Thich Nhat Hanh.

John has also been strongly influenced by the Theravadin school of Buddhism. As an organized "tradition," John has found these "teachings of the elders" to be as authentic as is possible today to what the Buddha likely taught, with little adornment or embellishment.

Also, in 1981, John was blessed to find a 12-Step based program, a program whose sole purpose is to provide a spiritual solution to addiction and alcoholism, which John suffered with from his youth. Over time John came to understand that the simple truths developed by the 12 Steps and the Eightfold Path to be mutually supportive in understanding self-centered views and realizing Right View.

John has found that the original and authentic teachings of the Buddha are found in The Four Noble Truths and that the path of lasting happiness and peace is The Eightfold Path. Mindfulness of life as life occurs within the framework of The Eightfold Path, including a true and effective meditation practice, are the keys to the Buddha's profound teachings.

Ultimately it has been through a well-concentrated and refined mindfulness of the Buddha's direct teachings of The Four Noble Truths and the supportive Sutta's of the Pali Canon that have proved to be most beneficial to John in developing understanding.

John teaches meditation within the context of developing an understanding of The Four Noble Truths so that all those drawn to this Dhamma will put aside disappointment and suffering caused by clinging, craving, desire, and aversion, and gain liberation from the distraction of Dukkha.

John writes a blog and produces recordings related to the teachings of the Buddha and teaches the Dhamma in weekly classes and residential retreats.

John is also available for private instruction for individuals as well as private groups.

More information on individual instruction or online instruction is here: http://crossrivermeditation.com/crmc/individual-instruction/

In 2014 John developed and teaches a meditation program within the framework of The Eightfold Path for Hunterdon Medical Center's Integrative Medicine Department in Flemington, New Jersey.

John in association with Moira Kowalczyk present One-Day 12 Steps workshops using these same spiritual principles so that those with compulsions and addictions may also come to understand the true nature of their own suffering and extinguish the cause of all addictions. Information on the 12 Steps Workshops is here: johnh12steps.com

John is also the author of the book The Spiritual Solution – Simple and Effective Recovery Through The Taking and Teaching of The 12 Steps, available at Amazon.com, Createspace.com, and Johnh12steps.com.

You can contact John and subscribe to his newsletter via his web site: CrossRiverMeditation.com

Glossary

Abiding: Enduring, Steadfast.

Abstaining: To hold back, reserved.

Aggregate: A collection of separate parts to form a mass.

Altruistic: Unselfish action for the welfare of others.

Ambiguity: Unclear, indefinite, ambivalent.

Anatta: Not a self. What the Buddha teaches that is commonly thought of as a self is not a self. The Five Clinging Aggregates.

Anicca: Impermanent, ever-changing. Uncertainty is an aspect of anicca.

Animate: To bring to life.

Ardent: Enthusiastic, Whole-hearted, Inspired, Earnest.

Brahmin: Religious teacher typically Pre-Hindu or Hindu.

Buddha: Also know as the Tathagata, the one who awakened and taught others to do the same.

Cessation: Temporary or complete stopping.

Dependent Origination: What the Buddha understood upon his awakening. From ignorance through 12 observable causative links suffering arise.

Dhamma: (Pali) Truthful teachings of the Buddha.

Dhammacakkapavattana Sutta: The Buddha's first teaching setting the wheel of truth (The Four Noble Truths) in motion.

Discernment: Analytical thinking resulting in conclusion. Can be used to further delusion or to develop understanding depending on intention.

Discursive: Aimless and repetitive thinking.

Disenchantment: No longer holding favor, an aspect of suffering or an aspect of wisdom.

Dukkha: (Pali) Disappointment, disenchantment, stress, suffering, confusion, impermanence, anatta.

Ehipassiko: (Pali) Come and see (for yourselves).

Eightfold Path: Right View, Right Intention, Right Speech, Right Action, Right Livelihood, Right Effort, Right Mindfulness, Right Meditation (Shamatha-Vipassana Meditation) The Buddha's path to awakening.

Equanimity: Mental and emotional stability and balance under all conditions.

Esoteric: Hidden or special, meant for a select few.

Fabrications: Creating a view from false information.

Five Clinging-Aggregates: Five factors that cling together forming the appearance of a self i.e.: form, feeling perceptions, mental fabrications, consciousness (discriminating thought). Anatta.

Four Noble Truths: The Buddha's teachings on the result of Dependent Origination. All of the Buddha's teachings were taught in the context of The Four Noble Truths.

Hinayana Buddhism: Most closely associated with the original teachings of the Buddha.

Insubstantiality: Lacking substance or

maintainability.

Mahayana Buddhism: A later developed form of Buddhism not directly taught by the Buddha. Tibetan, Zen, Chan, Son, PureLand are all sects of the Mahayana branch of modern Buddhism.

Mindfulness: To recollect or to hold in mind.

Over-Arching: All-inclusive, all-encompassing.

Pali Canon: The authentic preserved teachings of the Buddha (The Vinaya & Sutta Pitaka).

Pali: The language of the Pali Canon.

Phenomenon (a): The observable ever-changing nature of life including objects, views and ideas.

Pragmatic: Practical, useful.

Sage: A profoundly wise person

Samadhi: A non-distracted quality of mind, concentrated.

Sangha: Originally the group of monks and nuns who were disciples of the Buddha. A group of meditators.

Shamatha-Vipassana Meditation: Shamatha means quiet or tranquil abiding, Vipassana means insight or to gain insight. With Shamatha-Vipassana Meditation one quite the mind gaining insight into clinging conditioned mind. Most effective when practiced within the framework of the Eightfold Path.

Siddartha Gautama (Gotama): The Buddha's birth name.

Sukkha: Lasting peace and happiness, human flourishing.

Sutta: A direct teaching of the Buddha. Occasionally a teaching from one of the monks or nuns that were direct disciples of the Buddha.

Sutta Pitaka: The second book in the Pali Canon that preserves the original teachings of the Buddha.

Theravada (in): A modern form of Buddhism that in some respects remains authentic to the original teachings. See Vipassana.

Vipassana: A modern adaptation associated with Theravadin Buddhism with an emphasis on insight meditation and also incorporating aspects of modern Mahayana Buddhism.

Index

S

T

Endnotes

[1] Samyutta Nikaya 56.31
[2] Samyutta Nikaya 22.86
[3] Samyutta Nikaya 47.10
[4] Majjhima Nikaya 10
[5] Majjhima Nikaya 10
[6] Samyutta Nikaya 56.11
[7] Samyutta Nikaya 45.165
[8] Anguttara Nikaya 10.121
[9] Majjhima Nikaya 117
[10] Majjhima Nikaya 117
[11] Anguttara Nikaya 10.103
[12] Majjhima Nikaya 117
[13] Majjhima Nikaya 117
[14] Anguttara Nikaya 11.12
[15] Anguttara Nikaya 3.88
[16] Majjhima Nikaya 117
[17] Majjhima Nikaya 117
[18] Majjhima Nikaya 117
[19] Anguttara Nikaya 4.41

[20] Samyutta Nikaya 45.8
[21] Majjhima Nikaya 117
[22] Anguttara Nikaya 2.19
[23] Majjhima Nikaya 117
[24] Samyutta Nikaya 45.8
[25] Samyutta Nikaya 45.8
[26] Anguttara Nikaya 5.27
[27] Anguttara Nikaya 4.41
[28] Samyutta Nikaya 22.5
[29] Samyutta Nikaya 56.11
[30] Anguttara Nikaya 9.1
[31] Digha Nikaya 16
[32] Samyutta Nikaya 22.95
[33] Samyutta Nikaya 56.11
[34] Samyutta Nikaya 38.14
[35] Samyutta Nikaya 38.14
[36] Majjhima Nikaya 11
[37] Samyutta Nikaya 56.11
[38] Samyutta Nikaya 56.11
[39] Samyutta Nikaya 22.102
[40] Bodhi Sutta, Udana 1.1
[41] Majjhima Nikaya 2
[42] Samyutta Nikaya 22.59
[43] Samyutta Nikaya 12.2
[44] Samyutta Nikaya 12.2

[45] Samyutta Nikaya 12.2

[46] Samyutta Nikaya 12.2

[47] Samyutta Nikaya 12.2

[48] Samyutta Nikaya 22.46

[49] Samyutta Nikaya 56.31

[50] Dhammapada, v.46

[51] Majjhima Nikaya 11

[52] Samyutta Nikaya 22.48

[53] Majjhima Nikaya 72

[54] Majjhima Nikaya 11

[55] Majjhima Nikaya 75

[56] Majjhima Nikaya 49

[57] Anguttara Nikaya 5.57

[58] Anguttara Nikaya 10.176

[59] Samyutta Nikaya 22.102

[60] Anguttara Nikaya 6.46

[61] Samyutta Nikaya 12.38

[62] Majjhima Nikaya 19

[63] Anguttara Nikaya 6.63

[64] Anguttara Nikaya 5.51

[65] Majjhima Nikaya 43

[66] Samyutta Nikaya 2.1

[67] Samyutta Nikaya 35.28

Printed in Great Britain
by Amazon

42011997R00194